English for Academic Study:

Reading & Writing

Course Book

John Slaght, Paddy Harben,
and Anne Pallant

University of **Reading**

CALS
Centre for
Applied Language Studies

Garnet
EDUCATION

Credits

Published by
Garnet Publishing Ltd.
8 Southern Court
South Street
Reading RG1 4QS, UK

Copyright © 2009 University of Reading's
Centre for Applied Language Studies, The University of
Reading, and the authors.

This edition first published 2009

The right of John Slaght, Paddy Harben and Anne Pallant
to be identified as the authors of this work has been
asserted in accordance with the Copyright, Design and
Patents Act 1988.

ISBN: 978 1 85964 555 0

A catalogue record for this book is available from
The Library of Congress.

Production
Project manager: Simone Davies
Project consultant: Rod Webb
Editorial team: Penny Analytis, Jo Caulkett,
                       Emily Clarke, Chris Gough,
                       Fiona McGarry, Nicky Platt
American English
adaptation: Jennifer Allen, Arley Gray
Art director: Mike Hinks
Design and layout: Nick Asher, Sarah Church, Neil Collier
Illustration: Mike Hinks, Doug Nash
Photography: Corbis: NASA, Warrick Page, Radu
                       Sigheti, Lee Snider; Getty: Derek
                       Belsey, Keith Brofsky, Floresco
                       Productions, John Foxx, David
                       Sanger, Shaul Schwartz, Beowulf
                       Sheehan, Rob & Ann Simpson,
                       Inti St Clair, Travel Ink, Keith Brofsky,
                       PhotoAlto/Sigrid Olsson, David
                       Selman, Jack Star/PhotoLink, David
                       Sutherland. Corbis: Robert Essel
                       NYC, Jeremy Horner, Caroline Penn,
                       Michael Prince, Franco Vogt, Roger
                       Wilmshurst; Mike Hinks;
                       The United Nations.

Every effort has been made to trace the copyright holders
and we apologize in advance for any unintentional
omission. We will be happy to insert the appropriate
acknowledgements in any subsequent editions.

Printed and bound in Lebanon by International Press

Permissions

Acknowledgements

The Reading course has been developed to dovetail with the Writing course produced by CALS colleague, Anne Pallant. Anne has played a major role in reviewing material at every stage of development and helping refine the rationale behind the reading into writing approach.

Further significant cooperation in reviewing and editing the materials has come from present and former colleagues at CALS, particularly Ros Richards, Joan McCormack, Colin Campbell, Paul Stocks, Heather Bagley and Sarah Brewer.

In the production of the pilot editions, Paul Thompson contributed considerable IT support and Jill Riley showed great patience and good humor in her painstaking editing and typing.

Pre-sessional teachers in 2000–2005 gave invaluable feedback during trialling of the texts, tasks, and teacher's notes.

Many thanks to all the above and also to the many hundreds of students who have already worked with pilot editions of these materials.

A big apology to anyone I have omitted from this list.

John Slaght, Author, April 2009

I would like to acknowledge the important contribution of Ros Richards as the author of a report on the research literature on academic writing. Many of the principles of the course are based on the observations and recommendations in this report. I would also like to thank her for her valuable evaluative comments on the early versions of the material.

I would like to thank John Slaght for his collaboration on activities linked to the reading material.

I would also like to acknowledge the many teachers and students at the Centre for Applied Language Studies who have contributed to the process of piloting and evaluating this material, in particular Beverley Fairfax, Mary Ferguson, Helen Fraser, Emma Grenside, Belinda Hardisty, Clare McClean, Pete McKichan, Jane Short, and Sebastian Watkins. I would like to thank Clare McClean for her contribution to Unit 1 of phrases for making polite suggestions for Peer Feedback.

I would also like to thank the teachers and students at the Language Centres of the University of Surrey and Robert Gordon University who have also used this material and given feedback.

The author and publishers would like to thank Ron White for his contributions to some of the questionnaire on pp.83–87, and for the expressions of comparison and contrast (adapted from pp. 6–9 and 68–69, respectively) in Ron White and Don McGovern *Writing*, Hemel Hempstead: Phoenix ELT (1994).

The task on page 150 is taken from McGovern, Don *Reading*, Hemel Hempstead: Phoenix ELT (1994).

Anne Pallant, author, April 2009

Introduction

This book combines the two important academic skills of reading and writing, on the basis that reading is an essential component of writing development. Activities are designed for use with the accompanying extensive texts, taken from actual academic sources. The Reading and Writing sections of the book can be studied independently, or they can be combined to form an integrated program of study.

Reading: Texts have been chosen to simulate the reading you will have to carry out during your future studies. This section of the book also focuses on the way you will have to read: not only for comprehension, but to evaluate the usefulness of a text for the purpose of research, for example. This kind of reading involves techniques such as skimming, scanning, search reading, careful reading, and browsing. (See also the introduction to the Reading section on pages 9–11.)

Writing: This integrated approach to writing encourages the development of critical thinking skills, with an emphasis on adapting information written for one purpose to the purposes of the individual writer. These skills will be essential to your future studies, and are particularly important in the context of academic writing. (See also the introduction to the Writing section on pages 79–82.)

Unit topics covered in the texts and tasks include:
- Academic Achievement
- Early Human Development
- The Environment Today (Reading section only)
- Telemedicine (Writing section only)
- Statistics without Tears
- Human Activity and Climate Change
- The Global Village
- The New Linguistic Order

The book is organized as follows.

Contents
Reading

Writing

Texts

Book Map
Reading

Topic	Skills focus
† • Economics focus: On the move	• Deciding if a text is useful: predicting content
	• Word building from a text
	• Identifying the organization of a text: analyzing a text to establish the purpose
	• Writing a summary of part of the text: complete a model
	• Dealing with unknown vocabulary: identifying word classes and relative importance of lexis
	• Evaluating the level of content: identifying writer's attitude from a range of options
	• Reading for a purpose: identifying whether a text is suitable for the reader's purpose
	• Reviewing reading styles: reflecting on activities of the unit
1 • The influence of class size on academic achievement	• Predicting text content: reflecting on personal experience
	• Reading for a purpose: predicting content
	• Reading selectively: identifying whether a text contains useful information
	• Identifying the writer's purpose
	• Understanding referencing in texts
• A case study: Shining star	• Reading a text for closer understanding (1): activities to encourage close reading
• The Asian paradox: Huge class sizes, high scores	• Reading a text for closer understanding (2): activities to promote close reading
	• Thinking critically about the text: reflect on outcome of reading the three texts
	• Making use of the text: complete a written assignment
2 • Interaction between nature and nurture	• Accessing background knowledge: predicting content based on personal experience
	• Vocabulary development
	• Reading for general understanding: skim read to answer global questions
	• Developing further understanding
	• Understanding the main argument: identify the best summary
	• Note-taking from the text: summarizing specific aspects of the text
	• Developing understanding of the text: understanding sequences of events
	• Working with words from the text: classify words and discuss their relationships
• Capacities of the newborn	• Pre-reading discussion
	• Inferring meaning from the text
	• Summarizing information from the text (1)
	• Summarizing information from the text (2)
• Hearing, taste and smell	• Using background knowledge
	• Reading for a purpose and creating a summary
3 • Acid rain in Norway	• Raising text awareness: activities to elicit personal experience of topic
	• Taking information from displayed information: using headings, illustrations, etc.
	• Writing a global summary: compare individual work with model summary
• Skylarks in decline	• More global summary practice: compare individual work with model summary

Topic	Skills focus

Writing

Unit	Unit essay	Objectives
1 Academic Achievement	Writing an essay: *What are the aims of academic study and how can they be achieved?*	• Reflecting on how to achieve academic success: questionnaire 1.1–1.4 • Reflecting on issues in academic writing: questionnaire 1.5–1.8 • Overcoming difficulties of academic writing: reflecting on issues in writing • Acknowledging expectations of the reader: reflecting on issues in writing • Reflecting on different approaches to organizing ideas: planning and introductions • Evaluating writing
2 Early Human Development	Writing an essay: *Nature strongly influences early human development. Discuss.*	• Analyzing the essay title • Considering how to organize ideas • Choosing information to support ideas • Practicing how to write paragraph leaders
3 Telemedicine	Writing an exam essay: *As technology continues to improve, the range of potential uses of telemedicine will increase. Telemedicine will offer more beneficial applications in preventing disease than in curing disease. Discuss.*	• Understanding differences between writing assignments and writing for exams • Developing rapid analysis of essay questions • Making decisions about organizing ideas • Completing essays within a time limit
4 Statistics without Tears	Writing an essay: *Statistics should be interpreted with caution as they can be misleading; they can both lie and tell the truth. Discuss.*	• Organizing ideas in response to an essay title • Identifying useful information in a text • Ending paragraphs with an effective sentence • Writing concluding paragraphs
5 Human Activity and Climate Change	Writing an essay: *What role has human activity played in causing climate change?*	• Writing clear definitions • Supporting and developing ideas
6 The Global Village	Writing an essay: *Discuss the positive and negative effects of globalization on the world today.*	• Choosing patterns of organization: cause and effect • Incorporating information from research
7 The New Linguistic Order	Writing an assignment: choice of three titles	• Simulating a real essay assignment: preparation • Looking at other patterns of organization

Reading

Introduction

In this course you will be working on four main aspects of academic reading:
- reading for a specific academic purpose;
- working on effective reading strategies;
- detailed comprehension of sentences and paragraphs;
- text analysis.

1. Reading for a specific academic purpose

Here you will be concentrating on getting information from the text that will help you complete an academic task. For example, you may need to:

- complete an assignment on a specific question, for which it is necessary to combine information from various sources;

- get an introductory overview of a new topic in order to assist with listening to a series of lectures on that topic;

- add new knowledge about a topic to what you already know. This could be, for example, note-taking for future exam revision or simply reading a text and thinking about what you have read in order to understand the topic better.

2. Working on effective reading strategies

The main strategies we will be looking at are:

- **Skimming**

    This involves **looking at a text quickly** in order to do one or more of the following:

    - Identify what the text is about (the topic)
    - Identify the main idea of the text
    - Decide how useful the text is for your purposes
    - Decide how you will make use of the text

    Skimming a text might involve looking at some or all of the following features of the text:

    - Title
    - Section headings
    - Abstract or summary provided by the writer
    - First and last paragraphs
    - First and last sentences of intervening paragraphs
    - Topic sentences in each paragraph (see also Glossary: paragraph leaders)

    Another form of skimming is when you are previewing a book in order to decide how useful it is for your purposes. In this situation, you might also look at one or more of the following:

    - Information about the author and/or publication details
    - Contents page
    - Foreword and/or Introduction
    - Index

- **Predicting**

  Predicting means using what you already know about the topic, what you want to learn about the topic from the text, and what you have learned from your previewing in order to **guess what kind of information the text will contain and how useful it will be**. You will often be surprised how much you already know about a text before you even begin reading. Brainstorming your prior knowledge will help you to understand the text.

- **Scanning**

  Scanning involves **finding words** (or other symbols, such as figures) that have particular importance for you. When you are scanning, you already know the form of the words or symbols you are looking for. When you scan, you normally focus on small parts of the text only.

- **Search reading**

  Search reading means quickly **finding ideas** that are particularly important for you. This is different from scanning because you don't know the exact words you are looking for in advance and cannot make a direct match.

- **Identifying the main ideas**

  This involves **understanding the writer's main points**. It may be possible to do this quite quickly after skimming the text. However, with more difficult texts it may only be possible to identify the main ideas after more detailed reading.

- **Careful reading**

  This involves **reading slowly and carefully** so that you understand every word in the text (or the part of the text that you are most interested in). You might do this in order to understand the details of the text and also to infer meaning that has not been directly stated (see below).

- **Inferring**

  Inferring means **obtaining meaning from the text that the writer has not explicitly stated**. Sometimes the writer expects you to fill in blanks in the text in order for it to make sense. Sometimes you may wish to infer why the author wrote the text, i.e., the writer's purpose, and also the writer's attitude to what s/he is writing about.

- **Dealing with unfamiliar words**

  When you find a word you don't understand in a text, you need to **decide first whether it is really necessary to understand the word**. Perhaps you can understand enough of the text without understanding the word, in which case you can ignore it. Alternatively, the context in which the word is located may allow you to guess the meaning of the word well enough to continue reading. If neither of these applies, you may have to look up the word in a dictionary. If you find you are using a dictionary so much that you are prevented from reading the text at a reasonable speed, the text may be too specialized for you, and you should consider finding another one that deals with the same topic in a more generalized way.

  An approach to dealing with new vocabulary is to decide whether you:

  - *need to know the word now to help you understand the text and use it later under different circumstances*. In this case, you will need some way of recording the word, e.g., in a vocabulary notebook. You will also have to decide whether to rely on working out the meaning of the word from context, or whether you need to check in a dictionary;

  - *only need to know the word now to help you understand the text*. This is often the case with technical words or low-frequency words. These are words that are not often used in English, even by native speakers of the language, except for specialist reasons. Of course, if you are reading a text in your academic area, you will need to know certain specialist vocabulary. You will need to record this vocabulary as well as use it so it becomes part of your active vocabulary, i.e., words that you use to communicate effectively;

- *don't need to know this word either now or in the future*. If the word does not prevent you from understanding the rest of the text, you probably do not need to worry about it. If the word occurs several times, however, you may feel it is necessary to work out its meaning or look it up and record it.

3. Detailed comprehension of sentences and paragraphs

In an academic context, much of your reading work will involve dealing with complete texts and extracting information from them in various ways, i.e., reading purposefully in order to make use of content. However, in order to fulfill your reading purpose, you may sometimes find it necessary to have a very precise understanding of specific sentences and paragraphs. There may be obstacles to your understanding in terms of grammar or ideas, or the text's organization or a combination of these. This is one problem that this book will help to solve.

Detailed comprehension involves analyzing the relationship between ideas within a specific sentence or between a sequence of sentences of up to paragraph length—or even beyond. This precise knowledge might be required, for example, to infer meaning, to view the content critically, to enhance overall understanding or to formulate precise understanding.

4. Text analysis

It is often helpful to understand the way a text is organized in order to make the best use of it. The organization of a text can be considered at the global level; for example, the way that the text is organized into sections and paragraphs according to the purpose of the text and the type of text. In a report of an experiment, for example, it is very common to see the following pattern of organization:

- Title
- Abstract
- Introduction/background
- Method
- Results
- Conclusions
- References/bibliography

Another aspect of organization that can be useful to examine is how information is organized logically at the local level, i.e., within complex sentences or paragraphs.

As you can see, there are many different aspects of academic reading that we will be considering during the course. While it is important to be aware of all these different aspects, it is also important to:

- **develop a flexible reading style**. Becoming a better academic reader is not just about mastering different aspects of reading. It is also important to decide the best way to read a text depending on the particular academic purpose that you have for reading it;

- **remember that the more you read, the better you will read**. Regular independent reading outside the classroom is essential for any student wishing to develop reading abilities such as fluency, greater reading speed, vocabulary acquisition, and the strategies associated with successful reading.

You can improve your academic reading level by making decisions about:

- **why** you are reading;
- **what** you are reading;
- **how** you are reading;
- **how well** you are reading.

Task Introduction

This unit will help you:
- practice and review the reading strategies outlined in the introduction;
- develop strategies for deciding if a text is useful;
- build vocabulary through reading;
- identify a text's organization;
- write a summary as part of understanding key issues.

The topic of this unit is based on an article about international migration and the integration of labor markets.

Text i-1 | Economics focus: On the move (155–156)

Focus task

Imagine you are going to attend an economic history lecture about the link between migration and economic forces. This is a new subject for you, and you want to have some background information before attending your first lecture.

You have a number of articles on the subject, but you don't have time to read them all. You must therefore decide which ones to read. Text i-1 is an introduction to one of the articles. You have to decide whether the whole article would be useful. We will go through the stages that will help you make that decision.

Task 1: Deciding if a text is useful

1.1 **Read the paragraph in italics in Text i-1 (the introduction). Who is the intended reader?**

a) a business analyst

b) an educated general reader

c) an economics student

d) a historian

Write down one reason for your choice.

1.2 **Reread the paragraph in italics. What can you guess about the text content and the way it will be organized? Write down as many ideas as you can.**

1.3 Read Text i-1 and highlight any sections that are similar to the ideas you predicted.

Don't worry too much about difficult vocabulary at this stage, as you are reading for overall understanding. You will deal with some of the new vocabulary in Task 2. You will also be able to further check your predictions in the tasks that follow.

Task 2: Word building from a text

2.1 Find the word *immigration* in the subtitle of Text i-1. Scan the text to find other examples of this word. Note the line number and highlight any words that are connected.

2.2 Look for similar words such as *migration* (line 5). Use the three different forms of the word *immigration* you find to complete the table below.

Word used	Line number	Word class	Connected language
migration	line 18	noun	to restrict migration

2.3 Look at Ex 2.2 again. What verbs or adjectives could you form from the words you have used to complete the table? Write sentences to show how verbs or adjectives can be formed from the words in the table.

to migrate; people first migrated to America in the 17ᵗʰ century

Task 3: Identifying the organization of a text

3.1 Look at Text i-1. How is it divided? Where does this division occur? Discuss with a partner and then check with your instructor.

3.2 Look at the first part of the text (lines 1–98) and answer the questions. Discuss with your partner and then check with your instructor.

a) What is the main aim of paragraph 1?

The main aim is _____

_____

b) What is the main purpose of paragraphs 2–4?

The purpose is _____

_____

3.3 Look at the second part of the text. What is the main purpose of this part?

Highlight some words, phrases or even sentences in the text to support what you think the main purpose of this second part is.

The main purpose of the second part of the text is _____

_____

3.4 Discuss with a partner and then check with your instructor.

Task 4: Writing a summary of part of the text

4.1 Reread the first part of Text i-1 (up to line 98) on pages 155–156. As you read, underline any ideas that now seem clearer to you.

4.2 Now complete the summary below. Use one, two or three words in the blanks.

> There is a clear link between the history of migration to America and economic factors.
> At first, migration to America was very expensive and migrants were usually
> _____ or indentured laborers. However, as travel became easier,
> many more people _____ . This continued throughout
> _____ and early 20th century, but then war and
> _____ slowed down and even reversed migratory trends.
> After the Second World War, _____ increased again.

4.3 Reread the second part of the text. As you read, underline any ideas that now seem clearer to you.

4.4 **Now label the paragraphs A–E starting at line 100. Then match the summaries 1–3 to three of the paragraphs.**

1 ☐ Countries all over the world have experienced economic growth, and this factor is likely to encourage another wave of migration.

2 ☐ Countries with the greatest wealth are now in a position to be selective in the type of immigrant they want. This is good for these countries, but causes greater problems for the poorest, least-skilled migrants.

3 ☐ Both the immigrants involved and the countries where they migrate to can benefit from the migration of labor. However, at first, the workforce in these countries tends to suffer.

Task 5: Dealing with unknown vocabulary

This activity will help you practice the technique for dealing with unknown vocabulary described earlier in the unit. You may wish to reread the notes on page 10 before doing the task.

5.1 **All the following words and phrases appear in Text i-1. Which ones do you know already?**

makes plain (line 25); *harsh* (line 36); *indentured* (line 43); *slavery* (line 49); *falling* (line 65); *comparatively* (line 75–76); *net* (line 79); *feasible* (line 91); *expansionary* (line 124)

5.2 **Find the words in Ex 5.1 in the text and decide whether a, b, or c applies.**

a) you need to know the word now and, if you don't already know it, add it to your active vocabulary;

b) you only need to know this word now because it would prevent you from understanding the general meaning of the text;

c) you don't need to know this word or, if you don't already know it, add it to your active vocabulary.

> **Study tip**
>
> All words belong to a particular word class, such as *noun*, *verb* or *adjective*. This is sometimes referred to as a *part of speech*. Identifying word class can help you work out the meaning of a particular word.

Complete the table by placing a check (✓) in either column a, b, or c.

Vocabulary	a	b	c	Word class
makes plain				
harsh				
indentured				
slavery				
falling				
comparatively				
net				
feasible				
expansionary				

5.3 Look at the following extract from the text. Write the word class of the underlined words. Use the following abbreviations: n = noun; vb = verb; pron = pronoun; adj = adjective; adv = adverb.

> The <u>world</u> ⁽ⁿ⁾ <u>has experienced</u> ^(vb) a <u>new</u> ^(adj) era of <u>globalization</u> ^(—), <u>which</u> ^(—) <u>is</u> ^(—) <u>much</u> ^(—) <u>quicker</u> ^(—).

5.4 Now complete the final column of the table in Ex 5.2 by filling in the word class.

Carry out this task by finding the words in the text and working out the word class from their position in relation to other words and their function in the text.

Task 6: Evaluating the level of content

When deciding on the value of a text for your academic reading purpose, it is often useful to think about the writer's attitude to the topic and her/his purpose for writing it.

Study tip

Reading research is always more effective when you approach it as more than just a source of information, for example, by taking an interest in the writer's attitude.

6.1 What do you think was the writer's attitude and purpose when writing Text i-1? Discuss with a partner.

6.2 Bearing in mind your discussion in Ex 6.1, decide which of the following you most agree with.

a) to inform the reader about the topic

b) to persuade the reader to accept his or her opinion

c) to challenge ideas about the topic

d) to give a balanced opinion about the topic

e) to do all of these things

f) to do some of these things

6.3 Write down your conclusions about the writer's attitude and purpose.

My views on the writer's attitude and purpose:

Task 7: Reading for a purpose

7.1 Discuss the tasks you have done in this unit with a partner. Then decide whether you feel Text i-1 is suitable or not for your reading purpose, i.e., to get some background information before attending a lecture on migration and economic forces.

7.2 Summarize your answer in one sentence.

_____

_____

_____

_____

Task 8: Reviewing reading styles

8.1 In small groups or with a partner, discuss the following questions to help you reflect on the activities you have carried out in this unit.

a) Why is it useful to predict the contents of a text before reading it?

b) What are reading strategies? How can they help the reader?

c) What is global understanding of a text? Why is it useful to get a global understanding of a text?

d) Why is reading very slowly through a text word by word often an unsuccessful reading strategy?

e) Why is it often important to read only parts of a text?

f) Why is it useful to consider who the intended reader is before starting to read a text?

8.2 With the whole class or in small groups, discuss the suggested answers that your instructor will give you. Make a note of important ideas below.

_____

_____

_____

_____

_____

_____

_____

_____

Academic Achievement

This unit will help you:
- use your prior knowledge to help you understand what you are reading;
- practice reading for a specific purpose;
- make decisions about the relevance of a text in terms of reading purpose;
- read selectively in order to use appropriate information from the text.

The topic of this unit concerns factors that may lead to improvement in academic performance among students. It is based on three major research projects carried out in the United States.

Text 1-1 | The influence of class size on academic achievement (157–159)

Task 1: Predicting text content

1.1 Think about what factors can have an influence on the academic achievement of the students in a school, college, or university.

1.2 Look at the following list of possible influences and rate the ideas on a scale of 1–5 (1 = *very little influence*, 5 = *very strong influence*).

Influence on academic performance	Rating
Resources available (e.g., computers, laboratories, textbooks)	
Teacher level (qualifications, experience, etc.)	
Student motivation	

1.3 Add and rate some of your own ideas. Then compare your list and ratings with a partner.

Focus task

Your reason for reading Text 1-1 is to get some background information to help you write the following essay.

> What are the aims of academic study and how can they be achieved?

Task 2: Reading for a purpose

2.1 Look carefully at the title of Text 1-1. Do you think that the text will be useful for writing an assignment about academic achievement? Share your conclusions with another student.

2.2 Read the introduction to Text 1-1 (lines 1–66). As you read, try to make up your mind about how useful this text might be for your purpose. When you have finished reading, circle and complete the following sentence.

The text may / will / will not be useful because _____

_____

_____

_____

Task 3: Reading selectively

3.1 Read the subheading (lines 67–68) and think about your own opinion on the issue. Do you think that smaller class sizes help to improve academic performance? Circle your answer then write one reason for your choice below.

Yes / No / Not sure

_____

_____

_____

3.2 Below are some notes that have been made by another student on Text 1-1. Read lines 67–117 and check the points mentioned in the text.

a) ☐ easier to concentrate

b) ☐ students prefer smaller classes

c) ☐ more cooperative learning occurs

d) ☐ more help for students with problems

e) ☐ students develop good methods of learning

f) ☐ more opportunities to use resources if fewer students in class

g) ☐ students get much better academic results

3.3 Read lines 69–72. What does *anecdotal* mean? Try to guess the meaning of this word by looking carefully at the whole sentence.

If the ideas in this paragraph are *anecdotal*, think about how seriously you should take them into account when writing your assignment.

3.4 Read lines 97–117 and underline specific information from this paragraph that you might use to help in the completion of the Focus task.

Think about:

- how useful you think this paragraph might be in relation to the Focus task;
- whether you think the sources are reliable.

3.5 With a partner, compare and justify your choice of information for all four questions.

Task 4: Identifying the writer's purpose

4.1 Read lines 118–192 and decide on the main functions of this section of text from the choices given below.
For each choice, rate the function from 0–5 depending on how sure you are (5 = very sure).

Study tip

It can be very helpful to recognize why the writer has written a text, or a section of a text, i.e., what the function of the text is.

Function	Rating
a) To persuade the readers to accept a certain point of view.	
b) To explain the importance of using research data instead of *anecdotal* explanations.	
c) To evaluate the importance of the research carried out into the effect of classroom size on academic achievement.	
d) To describe the research method used in various parts of the US into the effect of classroom size on academic achievement.	

4.2 What is the function (or functions) of Figure 1: *Milestone studies in class size* (page 159)?

a) to summarize the content of the text

b) to outline the content of certain relevant research

c) to explain the importance of the STAR project

d) to compare the data from research about class size

Task 5: Understanding referencing in texts

Referencing in a text is a way of linking words and ideas together, thus making the text more cohesive and easier to understand. The following activity will provide practice in this important skill.

Study tip

An effective reader makes use of referencing in a text to gain a clear understanding of what the author wishes to convey.

5.1 Look at line 119 of Text 1-1. What information or idea in the text do the words *these findings* refer to?

a) The US Department of Education

b) The National Assessment of Educational Progress

c) Project STAR

5.2 What other words or phrases (lines 119–148) refer to the same data?

a) _____ (line number _____)

b) _____ (line number _____)

5.3 What reasons do the writers give for ignoring the data? Complete the list below, using a similar note form.

a) Decreased dropout rates

b) _____

c) _____

d) _____

e) More experienced teachers

5.4 What factors, according to the writers, made Project STAR better than other *poorly designed* studies? Complete the list below, using a similar note form.

a) _____

b) The research was carried out over a number of years

c) _____

d) _____

e) No new curricular methods

Text 1-2 | A case study: Shining star (p. 160)

Task 6: Reading a text for closer understanding (1)

6.1 What general point is made in the first paragraph of Text 1-2 (lines 1–11)? Find a short phrase that best summarizes this conclusion.

_____

_____

_____

6.2 In the second paragraph, which of the following benefits of smaller classes do Finn and Achilles (1990) identify in their review of the project? Answer *true* or *false* and add the line number from where you found the answer.

a) Better academic performance in small-sized classes. _____ (line number _____)

b) Students benefit at an early stage in small classes. _____ (line number _____)

c) Students later continue to perform well in normal-sized classes. _____ (line number _____)

d) Average students make the most progress. _____ (line number _____)

e) Minority groups gained the most significant benefits. _____ (line number _____)

f) On average, ethnic minority students improved by one-fifth of standard deviation. _____ (line number _____)

6.3 In the final paragraph, which of the findings of Finn and Achilles (ibid.) in Ex 6.2 does Hanushek comment on? Put a check (✔) when Hanushek agrees and a cross (✗) when he disagrees. Write *N/A* if Hanushek does not mention these findings.

a) _____

b) _____

c) _____

d) _____

e) _____

f) _____

6.4 To what extent do you feel that the analyses of Project STAR will help you with the Focus task? Rate your opinion 0–5 (0 = not at all). Discuss your answer with a partner.

Text 1-3 The Asian paradox: Huge classes, high scores (p. 161)

Task 7: Reading a text for closer understanding (2)

7.1 Discuss with a partner or in groups what you know about academic performance in developed Asian countries, and how academic success is achieved.

7.2 Read lines 1–65 of Text 1-3. As you read, remember to highlight ideas that might be useful for the Focus task.

7.3 What is your understanding of the "Asian paradox"? What one word in the text (lines 17–35) gives a reason for this Asian paradox?

_____

7.4 Find other short phrases in the rest of the paragraph (lines 35–48) that might provide further reasons for the apparent academic success of Japanese students.

_____

_____

_____

_____

_____

_____

7.5 Having read the text, have you found any information that might be useful for the Focus task?

Task 8: Thinking critically about the text

8.1 Look at the list of possible influences on academic performance in Task 1 (page 18). Are there any new influences you want to add to the table, and any you want to delete?

Influence on academic performance	Rating

8.2 If you added any influences to your table, what rating would you give them, on a scale of 1–5?

Task 9: Making use of the text

You now have some information that may help with the Focus task that you will be given in order to complete Unit 1 of _English for academic study: Writing_, if you are studying that course.

Decide now if, and how, you can use the information in Texts 1-1, 1-2 and 1-3.

Unit summary

In this unit you have thought about using your prior knowledge to help you understand what you are reading and made decisions about the relevance of a text in terms of reading purpose. You have learned to identify the writer's purpose and to read selectively in order to use appropriate information from the text.

1 **Complete this summary about the reading skills you practiced in the first unit with some of the words from the box.**

> understanding   expertly   prior   title   critically   predictions
> meaning   subheadings   selectively   purpose

It is easier to read a text if you have some _____ knowledge of the topic that the text is about. This will help you to make _____ and will give you a _____, which you always need when you read. Knowing why you are reading and what you are looking for will help you to both enjoy a text and focus on it better. Reading the _____ and any _____ there might be will help you to quickly know if you want to read a text and how useful it will be to you. It is important to read _____, especially if you are short of time. Some parts of a text will provide the information you need while other parts will be less important. You will usually read a text quickly first to get a general idea of what it is about and then read more carefully for closer _____ and to be able to think _____ about the content.

2 **Look at these possible topics of a reading passage. How much prior knowledge do you have of each topic? Mark each topic as follows:**

L – I know a lot about this topic, so I could make plenty of predictions.

S – I know something about this topic, and so I could make a few predictions.

N – I know very little or nothing about this topic, so I wouldn't be able to make any predictions.

a)   increasing traffic congestion in major cities

b)   special education for children with learning difficulties

c)   the growth in the popularity of baseball in Asian countries

d)   the intelligence of dolphins

e)   the origins of development of paper making

For web resources relevant to this unit, see:
www.englishforacademicstudy.com/us/student/reading/links

2 Early Human Development

This unit will help you:
- read about human development, focusing on the relationship between nature and nurture;
- learn how to make use of the knowledge you already have about a topic before you read more;
- recognize key words and find out the meaning of difficult/unfamiliar words;
- quickly identify the main points of the text that you are reading;
- read parts of a text more carefully in order to make use of it fully according to your purpose;
- practice summarizing useful information that you have found in a text.

The topic of this unit concerns human development at an early age, focusing on the relationship between *nature* and *nurture*.

Text 2-1 | Interaction between nature and nurture (pp. 162–163)

Task 1: Accessing background knowledge

1.1 **The following is the first sentence of a text about nature and nurture. Think about the information it contains and how it is connected with the picture. Then check which of a–d best represents what you know about this topic.**

> The question of whether heredity ("nature") or environment ("nurture") is more important in determining the course of human development has been debated through the centuries.

Atkinson, R. L. *et al*, *Hilgard's Introduction to Psychology*, 13th edition (1999). © 1996.

a) ☐ Nothing

b) ☐ A little

c) ☐ A moderate amount

d) ☐ A lot

1.2 **Check the statement that you think is most important in determining the course of human development.**

a) ☐ Nature (genes) is the most important.

b) ☐ Nurture (the environment you live in) is the most important.

c) ☐ Nature and nurture are equally important.

d) ☐ I'm not sure.

Task 2: Vocabulary development

2.1 **The lexical items a–t all occur in Text 2-1. Match with the definitions 1–20. Write the appropriate numbers in the boxes supplied. Use a dictionary when necessary.**

a)	nature	1		a baby before it is born
b)	nurture	2		the effect of one thing on another
c)	senses	3		an infectious illness
d)	malleable	4		egg
e)	heredity	5		to get faster
f)	personality traits	6		inborn, already present at the time of birth
g)	environment	7		inheriting characteristics from previous generations
h)	genetic	8		natural processes
i)	innate	9		permanent characteristics of somebody's behavior
j)	biological	10		processes caused by surroundings
k)	ovum	11		related to brain processes
l)	fetus	12		related to language, especially when it is spoken
m)	German measles	13		related to the mother
n)	maternal	14		relating to the information that is coded in the cells of the body
o)	interaction	15		to repeat a skill to improve it
p)	to practice	16		sight, taste, touch, etc.
q)	to accelerate	17		surroundings
r)	neurological	18		to bring up or educate (children)
s)	to rear	19		to do with the physical processes of living things
t)	verbal	20		very flexible and changeable

2.2 **The following two lexical items are defined in the text. Find them and write an appropriate definition for each.**

maturation (Paragraph D)

_____

_____

motor behaviors (Paragraph F)

_____

_____

Task 3: Reading for general understanding

Read through Text 2-1 to get a general idea about its contents. As you read, think about your answers to Task 1.

a) Does the text confirm or contradict your answer to Ex 1.2?

b) According to the text, which is a more powerful influence on the development of a child, nature or nurture?

Task 4: Developing further understanding

4.1 **Read Paragraphs A–C of Text 2-1. Which of the people in the box are connected with the following ideas? Some ideas may relate to more than one of them.**

> John Locke   modern psychologists   19th-century scientists   Skinner & Watson

a) Nature is more important than nurture in human development.

b) Human development is determined entirely by experience.

c) Human development can be easily influenced or changed.

d) Both hereditary and environmental factors are important in human development.

4.2 **Read Paragraphs D–H of Text 2-1. Which paragraph discusses the following ideas?**

a) The unchanging stages in the learning of motor skills.

b) Nature's role in shaping certain basic physical features.

c) The development of language skills.

d) The effect of environmental factors such as illness, or the habits of the mother on natural human development.

e) The effects of training on motor skills.

Task 5: Understanding the main argument

Read the following sentences and check the one that summarizes the main argument most accurately.

a) ☐ Most experts today agree that babies mainly develop as a result of the environment in which they live, and that the type of adult they become is determined by the early training they are given.

b) ☐ According to current opinion, a combination of natural development before and after birth, and the experiences that infants have, influence their processes of maturation.

c) ☐ Today, scientists believe that humans evolve into their final adult form as the result of biological processes that alone determine the development of motor skills and the ability to speak.

d) ☐ There have been many debates about the main influences on early human development throughout history, and even now, many scientists are unable to agree about this issue.

Task 6: Note-taking from the text

Imagine you are writing an essay about early human development. You have decided to include a table that summarizes the ways in which early human development can be influenced by nature and nurture.

Complete the table below, referring back to Text 2-1 as necessary.

Table 1: *The influence of nature and nurture on early human development*

Influences of *nature* on early human development	Influences of *nurture* on early human development
Genetic structure of fertilized ovum determines sex of fetus, color of hair, general body size, etc.	Abnormal uterine environment can affect maturation process, e.g., if mother contracts German measles.

Source: *Hilgard's introduction to psychology*, 12th edition by Atkinson. ©1996. pp 70–71.

Task 7: Developing understanding of the text

Read Text 2-1 again and choose the time periods from the box that correspond to the ideas below. Some ideas may relate to more than one time period.

> 17th century   19th century   1930s   second half of 20th century   20th century

a) Children's development can be completely shaped by training.

_____

b) If children are given practical encouragement, they will learn to walk more quickly.

_____

c) Human development only occurs after birth.

_____

d) The hereditary view supports the biological theory.

_____

e) Encouragement from people can speed up children's development of speech.

_____

f) Children have inherited characteristics that develop naturally after birth, but are not influenced by the environment.

_____

g) Environmental factors can affect human development before birth.

_____

Task 8: Working with words from the text

8.1 **Sort the words in the box below into word groups, e.g., parts of speech, similar meanings, etc.**

You may decide you need a number of different groups, and some words may come into more than one group.

| to accelerate   biological   environment   fetus   genetic
German measles   heredity   innate   interaction   malleable
maternal   nature   neurological   nurture   ovum
personality   traits   to practice   to rear   senses   verbal |

8.2 **Explain your word groups to a partner and establish which words do not seem to fit into any of the groups?**

Text 2-2 | Capacities of the newborn (p. 164)

This section concerns the capacities of newborn babies, still within the overall topic of early human development. There is a focus on search reading and summarizing useful information found in the text.

Task 9: Pre-reading discussion

In your opinion, how well prepared are newborn babies to learn from their environment? Which of the following do you think is most likely? Discuss your answer with your group.

a) They are poorly prepared and are totally confused by what is going on around them.

b) They are well prepared and are ready to learn quickly.

Task 10: Inferring meaning from the text

Read Paragraph A of Text 2-2 and answer the following questions.

a) What are the *sensory systems* (line 7) mentioned by the writer?

b) What is the writer's answer to the question in Task 9?

Task 11: Summarizing information from the text (1)

11.1 **Without reference to the text, consider the following questions.**

a) How do you think psychologists know that newborn babies are *well prepared to learn about their new environment?*

b) What kind of experiments do you think psychologists might have done to find out?

11.2 **Read Paragraph B of Text 2-2 to answer the following question.**

> In what ways have psychologists investigated how well prepared newborn babies are to learn from their environment?

a) Highlight the key words that give you this information.

b) Compare your key words with those of the rest of the class, and discuss why you have chosen them.

11.3 **Write a one-sentence summary using your key words, without referring back to the text. Then compare your summary with the rest of the class.**

_____

_____

_____

Task 12: Summarizing information from the text (2)

12.1 **Think about how young babies develop vision. Which of the following do you think are most visually attractive to babies?**

a) the center or edges of objects

b) patterned or plain objects

c) curves or straight lines

d) faces or machines

12.2 **Read Paragraphs C–E to check your answers to Ex 12.1. Highlight the key words that give you this information.**

12.3 **Write a one-sentence summary of the answer to the question in Ex 12.1 using your key words, without referring back to the text. Compare your answer with a partner.**

_____

_____

_____

Text 2-3 | Hearing, taste, and smell (p. 165)

This section expands on the capacities of newborn babies. There is a focus on search reading and summarizing text-based discussion.

Task 13: Using background knowledge

What can newborn babies do in terms of hearing, taste, and smell? Put a check (✔) against the following things that you think newborn babies (aged one month or less) can do.

a) ☐ Hear loud noises.

b) ☐ Turn their heads towards where a sound is coming from.

c) ☐ Correctly identify where a sound is coming from in the dark.

d) ☐ See the difference between a picture of a cat and a picture of a dog.

e) ☐ Hear the difference between two sounds that are almost the same.

f) ☐ Hear the difference between speech and non-human sounds.

g) ☐ Hear the difference between some sounds better than adults can.

h) ☐ Tell the difference between hot and cold food.

i) ☐ Taste the difference between sweet, sour, and bitter-tasting things.

j) ☐ Smell the difference between their mother's milk and milk from a bottle.

k) ☐ Tell the difference between the smell of a banana and the smell of a peach.

l) ☐ Tell the difference between a nice smell and an unpleasant smell.

> **Study tip**
>
> We all use our background knowledge when reading, but a good reader will make better use of this important resource. You often know more than you think about a topic, so always try to relate what you read to what you know —or think you know. (See *Study tip* on page 29 on inferring meaning.)

Task 14: Reading for a purpose and creating a summary

14.1 **Read Text 2-3. According to the writer, which of the activities listed in Task 13 can newborn babies do? Note down anything that surprises or interests you.**

_____

_____

_____

14.2 **Discuss in groups the things you have noted in Ex 14.1 above. Refer to the text in order to support your point of view.**

14.3 **Text 2-3 suggests that babies have four innate abilities related to hearing, taste, and smell. Write a short paragraph summarizing these abilities. The summary should paraphrase the explanation in the text.**

_____

_____

In this unit you have learned how to use the knowledge you already have of a topic before you read more about it, and to quickly identify the main points of the text that you are reading. You have also learned to recognize key words and why they are important for helping you to achieve your reading purpose, and practiced summarizing useful information that you have found in a text.

1 **Check the statement in each pair of statements that is true for you.**

a) ☐ It is easier to read a text if I already know something about the topic.

☐ It makes no difference whether I know about the topic or not.

b) ☐ It is usually confusing to read a text if I have previously read a text on the same topic.

☐ It is easier to read a text if I have previously read something about the same topic.

c) ☐ I appreciate why it is a good idea to read for general understanding before developing further understanding.

☐ I don't understand why I shouldn't look for the specific information I need right away.

d) ☐ Before reading a text, I find it helpful to learn key words and phrases related to the topic.

☐ I like to think about what words and phrases mean as I read the text.

e) ☐ I know that I will need to understand key words and phrases to use them to write a summary.

☐ I can write a good summary without worrying about key words and phrases.

f) ☐ I often understand all the words and phrases but don't really understand the main argument.

☐ I can usually understand the main argument without understanding every word and phrase.

2 **Look at the topics and the list of words and phrases that relate to them. Can you recognize the one word or phrase in each list that is likely to be key to the topic?**

a) heart disease   skeleton / cardiac arrest / hospital ward / optician / painful

b) English grammar   chapter / equations / data / verb tenses / literature

c) sports injuries   fracture / score a goal / disqualification / disappointing / transfer window

d) public transport   powerful / luggage / bus lanes / parking meter / overtake

e) recycling   electrical / luxury products / lead-free / waste disposal / ozone layer

For web resources relevant to this unit, see:
www.englishforacademicstudy.com/us/student/reading/links

3a

The Environment Today

This unit will help you:
- read quickly for global comprehension of the main ideas in a text;
- make use of your prior knowledge to help your global comprehension;
- identify key words to enhance quick global comprehension;
- think about what strategies to use for a specific reading purpose.

In this unit you will read two texts from British journals. The first is from an article in *Geographical Review* about acid rain, and the second is from the *Biological Science Review* about the decline of one particular bird species.

Text 3a-1 | Acid rain in Norway (pp. 166–168)

Task 1: Raising text awareness

Often it is useful to be able to summarize a text quickly and efficiently without carefully reading all or nearly all of the words in the text. When you want to do a global summary of a text, you need to focus immediately on the topic. The title should help. After reading the title, you may find that you automatically draw on your prior knowledge to bring what you know about the topic to mind.

1.1 **What is a global summary? Write a short definition.**

_____

_____

_____

_____

1.2 **Look at Text 3a-1. What is the title? You have one minute to write down anything you know about acid rain.**

_____

_____

_____

_____

_____

1.3 **You may also want to ask yourself questions about the title, e.g., *Is acid rain only important in Norway?* What other questions could you ask yourself about the title? Discuss your ideas with a partner.**

Task 2: Taking information from displayed information

Text 3a-1 contains quite a lot of *overt* or *displayed* information, e.g., apart from the title, there are also three figures, a table, and two section subheadings. Figure 1, for example, tells you that the use of lime to reduce acidification damage in Norway seems to have increased significantly between 1983 and 1995 (particularly after 1993). Therefore, certain key words may be useful here and in the other sources of *overt* information provided with this text. Terms such as *lime* and *acidification damage* are obviously important, and are phrases on which you might focus in order to gain a quick global understanding of the text.

2.1 Look through Text 3a-1. What new information (or words) do you learn from Figures 2 and 3, Table 1, and the two section subheadings? For example, what trends do the figures suggest?

Information source	New information or words
Figure 1	Very sharp rise in amount of lime used to reduce acidification damage, especially since 1993.
Figure 2	
Figure 3	
Table 1	
Section subheading A	
Section subheading B	

Study tip

Remember to make use of display information for raising text awareness before reading.

2.2 You have learned about how to quickly access information to help you form a global summary. Discuss what you have learned in small groups and complete the following list of points.

Ways of quickly accessing information about a text include:

- looking at the title
- _____
- _____
- _____
- _____
- _____

Task 3: Writing a global summary

When writing a global summary, concentrate on the main points. Write as accurately as you can, but your main aim is to communicate clearly what you understand to be the key points of a text.

3.1 **Read Text 3a-1. (Your instructor will set you a time limit for this.)**

3.2 **Write a single-paragraph summary of Text 3a-1. (Your instructor will also set a time limit for this task.)**

_____

_____

_____

_____

_____

3.3 **Compare your summary with the model supplied by your instructor.**

3.4 **Think about the strategies you used to carry out the task. Bearing in mind your instructor's summary, do you think your strategies were successful?**

a) Do you agree with your instructor's summary?

b) What strategies did you use to carry out the task?

c) Were the strategies successful?

3.5 **How do you rate your summary?**

a) Check the score that you think best describes it: 100% ☐ 75% ☐ 50% ☐ 25% ☐

b) If you had any problems doing the task, what were they? Choose from the list below.

- Difficulty with the topic
- Difficulty with the vocabulary and/or the language
- The way the text was organized
- Difficulty with the content of the text, e.g., ideas, hypothesis, concepts, etc.
- The length of the text
- Other reasons (not listed above)

_____

_____

Text 3a-2 | Skylarks in decline (pp. 169–171)

You now have a second text to summarize. This will give you an opportunity to put into practice what you have learned from this summary.

Task 4: More global summary practice

4.1 Read Text 3a-2, in the time limit your instructor gives you. You will not have time to read the whole text.

4.2 Write a one-paragraph summary, using your own words.

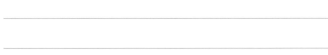

_____

_____

_____

_____

_____

_____

_____

_____

4.3 Compare your summary with the model supplied by your instructor.

4.4 Discuss the following questions.

a) In what ways was Text 3a-2 similar to or different from Text 3a-1?

b) What strategies did you employ to complete this task?

c) Were you more successful or less successful in completing the second summary?

Unit summary

In this unit you have practiced reading quickly for global comprehension of the main ideas in a text in order to write a summary. You have also thought more about how you can use prior knowledge to help your global comprehension and how identifying key words can enhance this.

1 **Complete this summary about accessing information in a text by using one word only in each space.**

If you want to access information in a text quickly and efficiently, you need to be able to quickly identify the _____ of the text—what the text is about. You won't need to understand the meaning of every _____ or phrase to do this. To start with, looking at the _____ of the text will help you to draw on your _____ knowledge and to start thinking about what the text might tell you. You might like to ask some _____ that you want the text to answer. Looking at displayed _____, like figures, tables, and subheadings will help you to make further predictions and build up a picture of the text before you read. As you read, you need to be able to identify _____ points that will help you summarize the main idea or argument in the text.

2 **In this unit, you had to identify the difficulties you had when writing a successful summary. Without looking back, complete this statement.**

My biggest difficulty writing a successful summary was _____

_____

3 **Give one piece of advice to a classmate who wants to write a successful summary of a text.**

For web resources relevant to this unit, see:
www.englishforacademicstudy.com/us/student/reading/links

4 Statistic without Tears

This unit will help you:
- practice reading to acquire knowledge;
- learn how to distinguish between main and minor points in a text;
- summarize information from short sections of a text.

The topic of this unit is statistics. Many classes involve some knowledge of statistics, either because these are often quoted in academic texts, or because students have to work with statistics for their academic assignments. Furthermore, governments and other organizations often use statistics as a basis for decisions that can affect all of our lives. From this point of view, some understanding of what it means to think statistically should be useful for everyone.

Text 4-1 | Making sense of experience (pp. 175–178)

Task 1: Statistics in practice

1.1 **Discuss the following questions in groups. Do you agree on the answers?**

a) Kate works in an office. On Monday, she arrived at work at nine o'clock. On Tuesday, she arrived at work at nine o'clock. On Wednesday, she arrived at work at nine o'clock. On Thursday, she arrived at work at nine o'clock. What time do you think she arrived on Friday? Why?

b) Your friend wants to show you a magic trick. He tosses a coin three times, and each time it falls to the ground with heads facing up. As he goes to toss the coin again, he asks you, *Do you think it will be heads again?* And you say *No*, but when he tosses the coin, it is heads. He tosses the coin twice more, and each time it is heads again. You pick up the coin and look at both sides carefully. What do you expect to see? Why?

1.2 **Are you sure you have given the correct answers in Ex 1.1, or could you be wrong? Is it possible to be absolutely sure about such predictions? Why, or why not?**

Task 2: Identifying main and supporting points

In Task 1, you used your everyday knowledge of the world to make judgments about what things are likely or unlikely to be true, in order to make a prediction about the current situation. This is an example of everyday statistical thinking. The text you are about to read looks at what it means to think statistically in order to make predictions. Don't worry if you find statistics difficult as the text is from a book called *Statistics without tears*!

2.1 **Read Text 4-1, Section 1. Which of the following are main points (write *main*) and which are minor points or examples (write *minor*)?**

a) We are naturally observant of the things around us. _____

b) Our observations often involve counting or measuring things. _____

c) Our observations may concern how big something is. _____

d) Sometimes our observations concern a single thing. _____

e) Sometimes our observations concern several things. _____

f) Observations may be made about a crop in a field. _____

g) We tend to look for connections among the things we have observed. _____

2.2 **Discuss your answers to Ex 2.1 with the rest of the class.**

2.3 **Look at the writer's question at the end of Section 1 (lines 29–30). Without reading further, write down what you think the answer is in one or two sentences. Compare your ideas with the rest of the class.**

_____

_____

_____

_____

_____

> **Study tip**
>
> It is sometimes useful to pause and think about what you have read so far. You will then be better prepared to understand information in the rest of the text.

Task 3: Continuing to identify main and minor points

3.1 **Read the first paragraph of Text 4-1, Section 2. How has the writer answered the question that was asked at the end of the previous section?**

It is important to fully understand the writer's answer, as this is a key part of what s/he wants you to learn from the text.

3.2 **Read the rest of Section 2. Which of the following are main points (write _main_) and which are minor points or examples (write _minor_)? Discuss your answers with the rest of the class.**

a) Statistics aim to help us make sense of our observations. _____

b) Statistics aim to help us avoid jumping to conclusions. _____

c) Statistics aim to help us be cautious about making generalizations. _____

d) A field was treated with a certain fertilizer and produced a big crop. _____

e) Perhaps other fields treated with the same fertilizer will produce big crops. _____

3.3 **Look at the writer's question at the end of Section 2 (lines 48–49). Without reading further, write down what you think the answer is in one or two sentences.**

_____

_____

_____

_____

Task 4: Summarizing the key points (1)

4.1 Read the first paragraph of Text 4-1, Section 3. How has the writer answered the question that was asked at the end of the previous section?

As with the answer to the previous question, this is an important part of what the author wants you to learn.

4.2 Read the rest of Section 3. Complete the following summaries of the main ideas in the text. Use a word or phrase from the box and write the correct number in each blank in the sentences that follow.

1	a certain kind of field
2	a mistake
3	correct
4	different kinds of fields
5	difficult calculations
6	likelihood (or "probability")
7	more confident
8	no 100% certainties
9	experience
10	more scientific

a) It could be __2__ to conclude that because one field produced a large crop, other fields treated in the same way will do the same.

b) The more observations we make, the _____ we can be about our generalizations.

c) _____ is a very important concept in statistics.

d) Likelihood (or "probability") refers to the idea that there are _____ in statistics.

e) _____ treated in a certain way may generally produce a bigger potato crop, but this may not always happen.

4.3 Discuss your answers to Ex 4.2 with another student.

4.4 Look at the writer's question at the end of Section 3 (lines 72–77). Without reading further, write down what you think the answer is in one or two sentences.

_____

_____

_____

_____

_____

_____

Task 5: Summarizing the key points (2)

5.1 Read the first paragraph of Text 4-1, Section 4. How has the writer answered the question that was asked at the end of the previous section?

5.2 Read the rest of Section 4. Complete the blanks in the following summary of the main points, using words from Section 4.

Statistics involves finding _____ patterns among things we observe.

However, we should not assume that _____ will all follow these patterns.

The two main concerns of statistics are:

● summarizing our _____ ;

● making _____ based on the reading summary.

Text 4-2 | What is statistics? (pp. 179–180)

You are going to read a second extract from the book. This has just one section.

Task 6: Concentrating on the main points

6.1 Read Text 4-2, Section 5, and make a list of the main points on a separate sheet of paper. You may find it easier to make three lists, following the divisions shown below.

Lines 90–109

Statistics is used in four different senses. _____

_____

_____

Lines 110–122

Most professional activities use statistical thinking. _____

_____

_____

Lines 123–140

Statistics is used because of uncertainty about our observations. _____

_____

_____

Descriptive and inferential statistics (pp. 181–183)

You are going to read a third extract from the book. This has just two subsections.

Task 7: Note-taking practice

7.1 **Read Text 4-3, Section 6. Look at the writer's question at the end of the section. Write down what you think the answer is, in one or two sentences.**

_____

_____

_____

_____

_____

7.2 **Compare your ideas with the rest of the class.**

7.3 **Read the first paragraph of Text 4-3, Section 7. How has the writer answered the question asked at the end of the previous section?**

7.4 **Read the rest of Section 7. Makes notes or annotate parts of the text to prepare for writing a summary.**

You are reading Section 7 to find out what the writer says about the distinctions between descriptive and inferential statistics, and the reliability of making generalizations.

7.5 **Write a short summary, using your notes from Ex 7.4.**

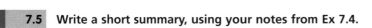

_____

_____

_____

_____

_____

_____

Task 8: Recalling information from the text

Recalling information that you have previously read is a useful strategy for improving your understanding of a text.

8.1 **Put away Text 4-3 and any notes you have made. With a partner, try to recall from memory the main points in Section 7, using the words in the box to help you.**

> descriptive statistics   inferential statistics   population
>
> generalization   sample
>
> observation   representative   reliability

8.2 **Check through the text to see if you have forgotten any important information.**

8.3 **Write a short summary of Section 7, using the following two headings.**

- Distinctions between descriptive and inferential statistics
- The reliability of making generalizations

_____

_____

_____

_____

_____

_____

_____

_____

_____

_____

_____

_____

8.4 **Discuss and compare your summaries in small groups.**

8.5 **Compare your summary with the one given to you by your instructor. Have you selected similar main points?**

In this unit you have practiced reading to acquire knowledge and learned how to distinguish between main and minor points in a text. You have also practiced summarizing information from short sections of a text.

1 **Divide the following words into two categories. Write them into the correct half of the box below.**

minor   main   key   supporting   important

2 **Look at these two topics and the list of points. Can you identify the ONE main point and the two supporting points in each? Check the main point.**

Growing populations in the world's biggest cities

a) ☐ Quickly built shanty towns have no electricity or hot water.

b) ☐ There are hundreds of thousands of new arrivals each month.

c) ☐ It is almost impossible to control crime in some of the poorest areas.

Sports injuries

a) ☐ Sports injuries can be broadly classified as either traumatic or overuse injuries.

b) ☐ A bruise is damage to small blood vessels that causes bleeding.

c) ☐ The inflammatory stage typically lasts about five days.

3 **Delete the wrong option in each statement below so that it is true for you.**

a) I find it *easy / sort of easy / sort of difficult / very difficult* to quickly identify the main points in a text.

b) I find it *easy / sort of easy / sort of difficult / very difficult* to distinguish between main points and minor points.

c) I find it *easy / sort of easy / sort of difficult / very difficult* to concentrate on the main points as I read.

d) I find it *easy / sort of easy / sort of difficult / very difficult* to summarize the main points of a text.

e) I find it *easy / sort of easy / sort of difficult / very difficult* to later recall the main points of a text I have read.

For web resources relevant to this unit, see:
www.englishforacademicstudy.com/us/student/reading/links.

5 Human Activity and Climate Change

This unit will help you:
- learn how to overview a text before reading, to assess its value;
- read selectively to identify words that might provide relevant information;
- practice *writing into reading* as a technique for increasing understanding of a text;
- identify topic sentences in a paragraph and recognize the supporting sentences;
- learn text-mapping as a means of enhancing understanding;
- make use of graphs, figures, and tables to increase understanding of content.

In this unit you will read three texts about climate change and whether man's activities have had a significant impact. The texts come from a brochure co-sponsored by the United Nations Environmental Programme (UNEP) and the World Meteorological Organization (WMO).

Text 5-1 Extra-textual information (p. 184)

Focus task

Your main reason for reading Texts 5-1, 5-2, and 5-3 is to prepare a set of notes using relevant information from the texts in order either to write an essay or to give a presentation about the following topic.

> What role has human activity played in causing climate change?

Before reading the text itself, you are going to look at some additional information included in the brochure, e.g., names of contributing authors and who they work for.

Task 1: Overviewing the text

The purpose of overviewing the text is to help make quick decisions about the particular value of the text to the reader. Overviewing saves time. Two ways of doing this are:

- to briefly look at any other extra-textual information, e.g., the blurb;
- to pay attention to the content of the Introduction.

1.1   **Can you think of other ways of overviewing the text? List them below.**

_____

_____

_____

_____

_____

1.2 Below is a list of questions that might be asked about a text before reading it. Find the answers by overviewing the whole document.

a) What is the text about?

b) Who is/are the author(s) of the text? What is their background?

c) Why was the text written?

d) What type of text is it?

e) Will the text be useful or relevant for carrying out the Focus task?

Text 5-2 Common questions about climate change (pp. 185–186)

This section of the text provides general information on the topic of climate change, including the role of human activity.

Task 2: Writing into reading

One effective way of fully understanding a text is to *write your way into reading*. This works by activating knowledge you may already have about the topic to help you improve your understanding of the text when you actually read it. *Writing into reading* involves writing down your own ideas about the topic, e.g., as a quick list, before attempting to read it.

2.1 Make a list of human activities that you think might have contributed to climate change. Check (✔) any activities that you have had personal experience of.

_____

_____

_____

_____

2.2 Compare your list with a partner and agree on a master list, i.e., the items on which you both agree.

2.3 Scan Text 5-2 and compare information in the text with your list.

Look for appropriate information about the impact of human activities on climate change.

Task 3: Identifying topic sentences

Paragraphs often contain a sentence that summarizes the main point of each particular paragraph. These are called *topic sentences*, and you can usually identify them through position and content. Topic sentences help the reader quickly grasp the main ideas in a text.

Discuss the following with a partner.

a) Where would you expect the topic sentence to appear:

- the first sentence?
- the final sentence?
- in the middle of the paragraph?

b) What is the function of the other sentences that appear in each paragraph?

Task 4: Understanding the general meaning of a text

4.1 Look at Paragraph A of Text 5-2. Pay attention to the sentence in lines 5–6. What are the issues? Number these issues (1–3).

4.2 Scan through the text and number the paragraphs 1, 2, or 3, depending on which issue they deal with.

4.3 Which paragraph(s) look(s) ahead to the future?

_____

4.4 What is the purpose of the final paragraph?

_____

_____

_____

_____

_____

Task 5: Topic sentences and supporting sentences

In this task, you will practice *careful reading* in order to differentiate the topic sentence from supporting sentences in each paragraph. *Careful reading* involves reading most of the words in the text in order to fully understand what is written.

5.1 Read Paragraph A. The underlined sentence is the topic sentence of the paragraph.

a) Why is this the topic sentence of the Introduction?

b) What is the purpose of the first sentence?

5.2 Underline the topic sentences in each of the remaining paragraphs (B–I). With a partner, discuss the role of the other sentences in each paragraph.

5.3 According to your understanding of the text, which of the following are main ideas (write A) and which are supporting ideas or details (write B)?

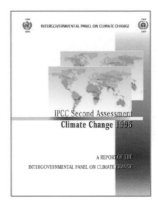

a) ☐ Rapid daily weather changes can occur even in areas of unchanging climate.

b) ☐ The Earth's surface temperature would be significantly cooler without a natural greenhouse effect.

c) ☐ The effects of the wind and the oceans determine the redistribution of heat over the Earth's surface.

d) ☐ Volcanic eruptions have a temporary cooling effect.

e) ☐ One of the causes of climate change is human activity.

f) ☐ The effects of natural greenhouse gases, combined with human activity, lead to higher average Earth temperatures.

g) ☐ The rise in the average global temperature will persist for a long period as a result of man's activities.

h) ☐ The Second Assessment Report released by the IPCC is very long and detailed.

Task 6: Recalling the text

This task involves recalling the contents of the text from memory. The idea behind this reading strategy is that after reading the text, you write down what you have understood from it. As a result, you may discover that you have understood more than you originally believed. Secondly, you will more easily recognize gaps in your understanding and recognize which parts of the text to concentrate on when rereading.

6.1 **Without looking back at the text, list the main points.**
Your instructor will only give you a few minutes to complete this task, so write quickly in note form.

_____

_____

_____

_____

_____

_____

_____

6.2 Compare your list with a partner and agree a master list, i.e., the items on which you both agree.

6.3 Check with the text. Revise your list if necessary.

6.4 Which of the points on your list are relevant to completing the Focus task on page 45? Place a check (✔) beside all the relevant points you have listed above.

Text 5-3 Are human activities contributing to climate change? (pp. 187–189)

This section appears to contain what you need to answer the Focus task, but you will need to confirm this.

Task 7: Identifying relevant information in a text

7.1 Read Text 5-3 to confirm whether it will help in the completion of the Focus task on page 45.

7.2 Reread Paragraph A. What do you consider to be the key point made by the author?

_____

_____

_____

7.3 What word(s) in Paragraph A suggest(s) that this claim should be taken seriously?

_____

7.4 Search through Paragraphs B–M and highlight areas of the text that might be of use in completing the Focus task. Use a pencil to check (✔) appropriate sections.

7.5 Which paragraph(s) in Text 5-3 give(s) a clear indication of the contribution of human activity to climate change? Note that there is, in fact, limited information about the importance of human activity in this text.

_____

_____

_____

> **Study tip**
>
> When highlighting a text, use a pencil rather than a highlighter because you may find you change your mind about the information at a later stage.

7.6 Now identify any paragraph in which the contribution of human activity to climate change is less clearly stated.
You will need to use inference to identify this information.

_____

_____

_____

_____

_____

Study tip

A lot of information contained in a text is implied rather than clearly stated. You will need to learn how to interpret such information.

7.7 In Paragraph B, what suggests the difficulty that scientists have in analyzing the problem?

_____

_____

7.8 In Paragraph E, what information might make the reader concerned about the way the data was collected?

_____

_____

7.9 In Paragraph K, what connection can be made between the comparison of _observed patterns of temperature change_ and those _predicted by models_ and the role of human activity on global change?

_____

_____

_____

_____

_____

_____

_____

Task 8: Detailed reading

A significant amount of Text 5-3 is not directly relevant to the Focus task, despite this being the main purpose for reading the document. However, it may be useful to study other parts of the text quite carefully to help your understanding of the topic.

8.1 An important function of Text 5-3 is to answer the question: *Are human activities contributing to climate change?* What other function(s) does the text have?

_____

_____

_____

_____

_____

_____

8.2 Complete the following summary by filling in the blanks with either one or two words. The words you need are all used in the original text.

Studying climate change

Studying the causes of unusual climate change is problematic because change caused

by _____ is often hidden or masked by natural climate

variability. In order to separate these two factors, investigations can be divided into

_____ and _____ studies. In the first case, information

can be gained by measuring _____, and in the second

situation by finding reasons for the unusual changes in climate that have been noted.

In attributing causes resulting from human activity, scientists can make use of

_____. Two examples of this are, first, by comparing maps or

patterns of temperature change, which is known as _____,

or second, by finding characteristic patterns of climate response between observed

climate change and predicted change from models, which is referred to as a

_____.

Task 9: Recalling the text from memory

9.1 Without looking back at Text 5-3, list all the key points (based on the main ideas). Write your list as quickly as possible, noting down the ideas as you think of them. You can rearrange these later if you wish.

Example: *Climate change caused by human activity, e.g., burning fossil fuels*

_____

_____

_____

_____

_____

_____

9.2 Compare your list with another student and agree on a master list. Place a check (✔) beside the key points you agree on. Refer to the text to consider any further key information that you have omitted.

Text 5-4 | What human activities contribute to climate change? (pp. 190–191)

Apart from the text, this section contains two figures (Fig 3.1 and 3.2). You can understand a great deal by carefully studying graphs, diagrams, illustrations, and tables. Such figures are intended to summarize the content of what you are reading.

Task 10: Making use of figures and tables

10.1 Study Figure 3.1 in Text 5-4. With a partner, discuss what conclusions can be made from this diagram. For example:

a) Compare the relative importance of climate change caused by carbon dioxide and by methane.

b) Discuss what contributions the greenhouse gases described in Figure 3.1 have made to climate change.

> **Study tip**
>
> By paying attention to the visual aids such as graphs, diagrams, and illustrations, you will get a much clearer understanding of the text.

10.2 To what extent does the displayed data in Figure 3.1 help you to answer this question?

> *What human activities contribute to climate change?*

10.3 Read through Text 5-4 and locate the sections that refer to each of the gases displayed in Figure 3.1. Underline the names of the gases as you locate them.

Task 11: Reading displayed information

Study Figure 3.2. What conclusions can be made about the contents of this figure? Answer the following questions to help you make appropriate conclusions.

a) What is the general trend for all three groups of countries?

_____

_____

_____

b) Which group of countries was contributing the most to climate change by 1992?

_____

_____

_____

c) What future trends are suggested by the graph? Read through Text 5-4 to find which paragraph(s) are related to Figure 3.2.

_____

_____

_____

Task 12: Inferring meaning from a text

12.1 **Reread Text 5-4 and find references to the following phrases. What is their significance regarding climate change?**

Example: The burning of fossil fuels = *very significant contributor to carbon dioxide emissions*

a) The regrowth of vegetation in the Northern hemisphere

b) Land use changes

c) Existing international agreements

d) The tropospheric zone

e) The Antarctic ozone hole

f) Small particles in the atmosphere

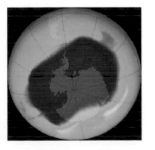

12.2 What general conclusions can be made about Text 5-4? Write your conclusions below.

_____

_____

_____

_____

_____

_____

_____

_____

_____

_____

_____

_____

Task 13: Making use of a text

You should now be ready to return to the Focus task on the first page of this unit (page 45). Reread this task and decide what information you can use from the three texts in order to prepare notes for an oral presentation, or a plan for a writing assignment.

13.1 Prepare and organize your notes as directed by your instructor.

13.2 Explain the contents and organization of your notes to a partner.

13.3 Give an oral presentation or complete a writing assignment, whichever your instructor assigns.

Unit summary

In this unit you have learned how to overview a text to assess its particular value. You have practiced reading for a specific purpose and reading selectively to identify words that might provide information relevant to a specific purpose. You have also practiced strategies to improve reading comprehension, which include writing into reading, identifying topic sentences and supporting sentences, text-mapping, and making use of displayed information.

1 Cover Ex 2 and answer these questions as quickly as you can.

a) What do you do if you *overview a text*?

b) What does *writing your way into reading* mean?

c) What is a *topic sentence*?

d) What are *supporting sentences*?

e) What is *text-mapping*?

2 Match the sentence beginnings a–h with the sentence endings 1–8.

a) ☐ If I overview a text, it will …

b) ☐ If I ask questions about a text before I read, it will …

c) ☐ If I practice *writing into reading*, it will …

d) ☐ If I look carefully at displayed information like graphs and tables, it will …

e) ☐ If I can quickly identify topic sentences, it will …

f) ☐ If I can differentiate between topic sentences and supporting sentences, it will …

g) ☐ If I write down key points from a text after I have read it, it might …

h) ☐ If I use a pencil to highlight points in a text, it will …

1 make me realize that I understand more than I thought and help me to identify what I didn't understand.

2 help me to summarize in a way that I might not be able to do by reading the text alone.

3 help me to activate prior knowledge and to understand more of the content.

4 help me decide what I want to find out from reading it.

5 save time and help me to make quick decisions about its particular value.

6 be easier to go back and make changes if I need to.

7 help me read more carefully and to understand the organization of a paragraph better.

8 help me know what information is key and what is detail.

For web resources relevant to this unit, see:
www.englishforacademicstudy.com/us/student/reading/links

The Global Village

This unit will help you:
- practice recognizing main points in a text;
- read for a specific purpose;
- analyze the titles, subtitles (subheadings), and other displayed accompanying information;
- recall the text to consolidate your understanding;
- compare your views (as a reader) with those of the writer;
- monitor your understanding of the text while you are reading.

In this unit you will read up to six sections of a text called *The global village* about the effects of globalization on the world we live in.

Text 6-1 | Introduction (pp. 192–193)

This introduction will give you an overview of the text.

Task 1: Pre-reading discussion

1.1 **The term *global village* was first used by the Canadian academic Marshall McLuhan.**

a) Discuss in groups what this term might mean.

b) Compare your group's definition with your instructor's definition. How similar are they?

1.2 **Consider some of the characteristics of the *global village* from your instructor's definition. Make a list of the ways that you think they may have affected your life.**

Example:

> You are studying abroad, and you may consider this to be a direct (or indirect) result of globalization.

1.3 **Compare your list with other members of your group.**

Task 2: Checking predictions

2.1 **Read Text 6-1. Are any of the points mentioned by the author similar to the points you listed in Ex 1.2?**

As you read:
- underline with a <u>solid line</u> any ideas in the text that are similar to the ones that you have on your list;
- underline with a <u>broken line</u> any ideas in the text that are not on your list.

2.2 **Compare your list with a partner.**

Text 6-2 | The shrinking planet (pp. 194–195)

This is the first of five sections and it will provide you with information on one aspect of the global village.

Task 3: Thinking about the topic

3.1 **The title of Text 6-2 is *The shrinking planet*. What do you think this means?**
Remember that the overall theme of the text is *The global village*.

_____

_____

_____

_____

3.2 **In what ways do you think trade, tourism, and technology lessen the differences between people in different parts of the world?**

Global brand names, e.g., Coca–Cola _____

_____

_____

_____

_____

3.3 **Think about the effects of globalization on the differences between cultures around the world.**

a) Do you think that some differences between people in different parts of the world may be maintained in spite of globalization, or even increased because of it?

b) If so, what examples can you think of?

_____

_____

_____

_____

3.4 Look at the words and expressions from Text 6-2 in the box below. Make sure you understand what they mean, using a dictionary if necessary.

> ~~discontent~~   cultural convergence   the Internet   grievances
> alien modern cultures   universal links   superficial   national culture, history, and language
> common interests   similar products   human peculiarities   homogenizing effect
> customization of products   local requirements   digital technology

3.5 Place the words and expressions in the appropriate column in the table below.

For example, *discontent* would probably cause *divergence*.

Convergence	Divergence
	discontent

3.6 In groups, discuss what you think the text will be about.

Task 4: Recalling the text from memory

4.1 Read the subheading of Text 6-2 and answer the following questions.

a) What is the function of this subheading and what does it mean?

_____

_____

_____

_____

_____

b) What contrast is suggested by this subheading?

_____

_____

_____

_____

_____

4.2 Read Text 6-2. Why does the writer feel that *many cultural differences persist*?

4.3 Work in pairs and recall the text from memory by telling each other what you remember. Some of the words and expressions in Ex 3.4 may help you.

4.4 Reread Text 6-2 to check your answers to Ex 4.3. Did you forget any important points? Were there any inaccuracies?

Task 5: Checking the text for details

This task will help you have a more detailed understanding of the text.

Read Text 6-2 again, then annotate the statements below as follows.

- If the statement is correct according to the text, write *Yes*.
- If the statement is not correct, write *No*.
- If you cannot find any information relating to the statement, write *Not given*.

a) _____ A surprising number of people in the world are able to watch TV.

b) _____ In 1998, Ronaldo, a young Brazilian footballer, was much better known internationally than President Clinton.

c) _____ Increasing numbers of Africans are migrating to the United States.

d) _____ Some people use the Internet as a method for making political protests.

e) _____ Books about Canada are frequently written in Spanish.

f) _____ There is a football team in Tanzania that has adopted the name Manchester United.

g) _____ An increasing number of young people in China have little or no knowledge of their national heritage.

h) _____ As a result of computer technology, more and more people throughout the world are driving exactly the same basic model of car.

i) _____ Digital technology seems to be reversing the effect of globalization.

j) _____ The writer is negative about the effects of globalization.

Task 6: Making use of the text content

6.1 **Discuss the following question in groups, and note the results of your discussion in the table below.**

The data you gather may be useful in carrying out the summarizing activity that is introduced in the next task (on page 61).

> Assuming that you are part of the global village, what cultural differences persist in your class (if any)?

Attitude about:	The same attitude?	Different attitude?
Study methods		
Studying abroad		
Entertainment		
Foreign goods		
International languages		
National culture		

6.2 **What conclusions can be drawn from the information you collected in Ex 6.1?**

Focus task

The aim of this Focus task is to provide an overall purpose for using *all* the texts in this unit. It will provide practice in making decisions about what to read and how carefully to read it. It will also provide an opportunity to practice your note-taking techniques. The topic is:

> Has social diversity generally increased as the result of economic globalization?

Based on your own experience and the experience of other members of your group, to what extent do you agree that social diversity has generally increased? What evidence exists in the texts to support your answer?

Task 7: Reading for a purpose

7.1 Think about the Focus task and decide on the most appropriate way to carry out this task. Discuss your ideas in small groups.

7.2 Look through Texts 6-1 to 6-6 (including any texts not yet referred to) and decide which parts of each text you could use to complete this assignment.
Remember to look for relevant information.

7.3 Underline ideas in each text that appear to *support* the statement with a <u>solid line</u>. Underline ideas that *do not support* the statement with a <u>broken line</u>.

7.4 Think about what should be included in the summary. What ideas have the title of the assignment and your reading of all the texts given you? Individually, or in groups, make a list of points to include in the summary.
Remember to consider the data you collected in Ex 6.1.

_____

_____

_____

_____

_____

Text 6-3 Economic globalization (pp. 195–197)

Task 8: Asking questions about the text

The aim of this section is to look more closely at Text 6-3 and decide how relevant the content is with regard to completing the Focus task. This is also an opportunity to reconsider the highlighting/note-taking you did in Task 7. You might want to change or add to your highlighting as you go through Text 6-3.

8.1 Look at the following questions. Read Text 6-3 and underline the words or phrases that answer these questions.

a) What inconsistency is expressed in the section entitled *The global marketplace*? (Use no more than ten words.)

b) What two things have increased dramatically because of economic globalization?

c) What two services, mentioned in Paragraph B, have been globalized?

d) What three international agreements and organizations have affected economic globalization?

e) What four factors have hampered economic globalization?

> **Study tip**
>
> One way of getting a better understanding of the text when reading carefully is to ask yourself questions about the text as you read.

f) What is done in some countries to protect the workforce?

g) Why does the expansion of international trade cause even some well-managed businesses to fail?

h) In what ways is the pre-industrial village different from the global village? (Use no more than ten words.)

i) Which countries benefit most from economic globalization?

j) In what three ways has economic globalization had a negative effect on richer countries? (Use no more than ten words per point.)

k) What positive long-term factors does the writer identify in the final paragraph?

8.2 **Can you think of any other questions you could ask that would help you understand the text?**

_____

_____

_____

_____

_____

8.3 **With a partner, decide how relevant your answers to Ex 8.1 are to the Focus task.**

Task 9: Identifying key information in the text

This task will help you check your understanding of the main point of each paragraph in Text 6-3.

Sentences 1–8 below summarize Paragraphs A–H of Text 6-3. Match each of these sentences with the appropriate paragraph letter from the text.

A = ☐ B = ☐ C = ☐ D = ☐

E = ☐ F = ☐ G = ☐ H = ☐

1   There are a number of factors that may delay the process of globalization.

2   The differences between people become less important as a result of economic globalization.

3   Several corporate household names exemplify current global trends.

4   International free trade is directed by global agreements and covers a far greater range of commodities than was traditional.

5   The developed world continues to dominate the process of globalization.

6   Economic power does not necessarily dictate policy when human issues stand in its way.

7   The size of foreign investment and the globalization of service industries are clearly demonstrated in most areas of the world.

8   Concentration of economic power is tending to cause greater tension between the rich and the poor.

10.1 Review the answers to Tasks 8 and 9.

10.2 Revise your list of points relevant to the Focus task (Ex 7.4). Add any new points you have found to your list.

10.3 In groups, compare your lists. Refer to the text where necessary to check your points.

Text 6-4 | Community & conflict (pp. 198–200)

The next text consists of a main body text (Paragraphs A–H) and three short accompanying texts that provide further comment about the topic. These are in separate boxes.

Task 11: Thinking about the topic

The text outlines some of the social effects that globalization has on individual societies. It will be helpful to discuss what you know about this subject before reading the next section.

11.1 Think about the title of Text 6-4: *Community & conflict*. What does this suggest about the contents of the text?

_____

_____

_____

11.2 Make a list of five causes of conflict in modern society on an international/global scale.
Example:

border disputes between two countries where one or both countries accuse the

other of stealing some of their land.

_____

_____

_____

_____

11.3 What "community" do you think the writer is referring to in the title of Text 6-4? Read the subtitle and the note *Global village—global inequality*. What implication is made regarding the possibility of conflict?

_____

_____

_____

Task 12: Developing understanding of the text

12.1 Read the subtitle of Text 6-4. Who are the citizens of the global village? Read Text 6-4 and highlight any words or phrases that might indicate certain characteristics or features of the typical *citizen*.

Example: *better educated*

12.2 Make brief notes on the types of global community mentioned in Text 6-4.

_____

_____

_____

_____

Task 13: Identifying relevant information for the Focus task

You will have to decide whether the contents of Text 6-4 are relevant to the Focus task assignment (page 60). But first you have to evaluate what it has to say about conflict, the heading of this section.

13.1 Read through Text 6-4 and highlight or annotate sections of the text that relate to conflict.

13.2 Compare your annotations with the list you compiled for Ex 11.2. Decide whether the points on your list are similar to the points raised in the text. Discuss the points listed in groups.

13.3 Decide whether Text 6-4 is relevant to the Focus task (page 60). Do you think that the social diversity mentioned in Text 6-4 is a result of economic factors?

13.4 Think about the causes of conflict mentioned in the text that you have already annotated. In what ways, if any, are the points you highlighted in Ex 13.2 related to economic globalization?

13.5 In groups, list any points that you consider relevant to the Focus task. Compare your answers with another group.

_____

_____

_____

_____

_____

Task 14: Completing an assignment

14.1 Write a two-paragraph summary of the main ideas you would use to complete the following assignment.

> Has social diversity generally increased as a result of economic globalization?
>
> To what extent do you think social diversity has increased? What evidence exists with reference to the texts selected from The global village: Challenges for a shrinking planet?

You might want to make use of the following techniques.

- Recalling the texts immediately after reading them to check your understanding.
- Asking yourself questions as you read through the texts, as you practiced with Text 6-3.
- Identifying topic sentences or main ideas as you read.
- Skimming through the texts first and then reading them more carefully (or selected parts that seem more relevant) and annotating certain key ideas or words.

Text 6-5 The sharing of sovereignty (pp. 200–202)

Text 6-6 Converging or diverging? (pp. 203–205)

These are two more texts from the same source that follow Text 6-4.

14.2 Read Texts 6-5 and 6-6 and decide whether or not these will be useful to you in completing the Focus task.

You will find it useful when reading and thinking about these texts to employ some of the reading strategies that you have practiced in this unit and in earlier units.

Unit summary

In this unit you have learned how to apply the reading skills you have learned so far to reading with the aim of selecting key information from a number of sources. You have also learned how to monitor your understanding of the text while you are reading, and you have compared your views (as a reader) with those of the writer.

1   **Use your notebook to write one thing that you think you have improved and one thing that you still find difficult when you are trying to apply each of the following reading strategies.**

    a)   making predictions about the content of a text

    b)   learning key vocabulary that will occur in a text before reading the text

    c)   reading for detailed information

    d)   recalling the text from memory

2   **Which of the following reading strategies did you find especially helpful when selecting information from a number of sources in order to complete the Focus task? Check three.**

    ☐   overviewing each text before reading

    ☐   asking yourself questions about the content of each text before reading

    ☐   making predictions about the content of each text before reading

    ☐   skimming each text quickly before reading more carefully

    ☐   highlighting points in each text in different ways (solid line / broken line, for example)

    ☐   writing down a list of key points from each text

    ☐   asking yourself questions about the text as you read

    ☐   trying to recall key points from each text before reading again to check

3   **Complete the following summary with some of the words from the box.**

> If the Focus task asks you to express an opinion, you will need to select
> _____ information from the texts you read that _____
> your answer. If you choose to express an opinion based on your own _____
> or that of people you know, you will need to make sure that you provide
> _____ to back up what you say.

> logic   essential   evidence   convince   relevant   experience   support

For web resources relevant to this unit, see:
www.englishforacademicstudy.com/us/student/reading/links

7 The New Linguistic Order

This unit will help you:
- read an article on "the new linguistic order" and use it to complete an assignment;
- practice making use of a specific text to support your ideas;
- develop the skills you have learned so far on this reading course.

In this unit you will read an article that appeared in the American journal *Foreign Policy*. You will make use of the contents of the article to complete an assignment. You will therefore be approaching the text in the same way as you will be expected to on many academic courses, i.e., *reading to learn* rather than *learning to read*.

Reading assignment

> What future significant language developments might occur in a country such as Zambia?

Discuss this topic with special reference to Text 7-1: *The new linguistic order*.

Task 1: Deciding how to read a text

You will have to make certain decisions about how to approach Text 7-1. For example, you need to be selective about the information that you will use. Obviously, the information should be relevant to the Focus task. This should lead you to make decisions about the text.

- Should you read the whole text first before making any notes, or should you annotate the text as you read?
- Should you look quickly at the headings in the text and read only the parts that seem relevant to the assignment?
- Should you look up every word you don't understand? If not, how should you deal with unknown vocabulary?

   Individually or in groups, make a list of other decisions you need to make about how to read the text.

Task 2: Reading an introductory case study

Before reading the main article, you are going to read a short text and discuss the importance of English in Zambia and the future English will have in countries like Zambia. This short text provides some background information relevant to the current use of English in Zambia.

2.1 **Read through the introduction to the text on page 68 and note down four points about the language situation in Zambia that you consider to be particularly important.**

LANGUAGES IN ZAMBIA

Zambia is a developing landlocked country situated in Central Africa. The population, approximately 9.7 million, is made up of 98.7 percent African people, 1.1 percent European and 0.2 percent other (*The World Factbook*, 1999—Zambia). The African population consists of four main tribal groups. There are also a number of subsidiary groups. As a result, there is a wide variety of tribal languages and dialects. There is also a significant number of other permanent residents in Zambia whose first language is not a Zambian tribal language or dialect. For example, there are first-language speakers of English, Swahili, Hindi, and Afrikaans. Because of this, it has been necessary for Zambia to have a common language of communication for a range of social, political, educational, technical, and economic reasons. Zambia is part of Anglophone Africa, and therefore the common language (lingua franca) is English. Approximately 78 percent of the population over the age of 15 can read and write English. There are also at least seven major dominant vernacular languages and approximately 70 other indigenous languages.

Zambia is surrounded by neighboring countries, each having a major European lingua franca as well as official tribal languages. These countries are Tanzania, Malawi, Zimbabwe, and Namibia, where the lingua franca is English; Angola and Mozambique (Portuguese), and the Democratic Republic of Congo (formerly Zaire), where the lingua franca is French. In all these countries, therefore, like Zambia, there is multilingualism, e.g., Zambians communicate through the lingua franca as well as through at least one of the official vernacular languages. Several of the local languages transcend borders. For example, Bemba is spoken in Northern Zambia and in the south of the Democratic Republic of Congo; Nyanja in Eastern Zambia and Malawi, etc.

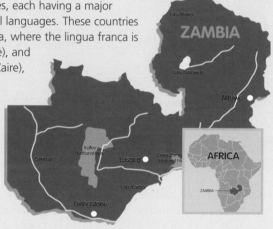

2.2 In groups, compare the points you noted in Ex 2.1. Discuss the possible significance of the following.

- The existence of other lingua francas on Zambia's borders.
- Local languages that overlap the borders of Zambia and her neighbors.
- Local languages that continue to be spoken by the vast majority of Zambians.

2.3 Look at the following possible developments and prioritize them in order from 1 to 5 (1 = *most likely*, 5 = *least likely*). In groups, discuss the order you have chosen.

IN THE FUTURE

☐ English will take over entirely as the only language spoken in Zambia.
☐ Language conflicts will develop between English speakers and other language communities.
☐ English will increasingly become the language of the elite, and non-fluent speakers will be seriously disadvantaged.
☐ The situation is likely to remain as it is, i.e., multilingualism with languages coexisting in order to serve different purposes.
☐ English will be replaced by some other official language.

Text 7-1 | The new linguistic order (pp. 206–214)

You are now going to read Text 7-1. As you read, you will need to think about what information would be relevant for completing the following assignment:

> What future significant language developments might occur in a country such as Zambia?

You will need to make notes as you are reading and will have to make decisions about how to do this. By the end of the unit, you will be expected to have produced notes on part of the text relevant to the assignment.

Tasks 3 and 4 will make use of the first part of the text in shorter stages before the main reading focus in Task 5.

2.4 **Read Text 7-1. As you read, think about what information would be relevant to the Focus task and make notes.**

Task 3: Understanding subject-specific vocabulary

It is normal in an academic situation for a student to have a working vocabulary of a particular subject or topic that has been learned either in class or from reading subject materials. Such a working vocabulary of subject-specific words should help the reader understand any relevant text they are asked to read.

3.1 **Read Paragraphs A–C and find the words or phrases in the box. Then match them with the definitions a–e below.**

> **1** mother tongue **2** globalization **3** official language
>
> **4** regionalization **5** local language

a) ☐ A process in which a language is used in neighboring countries, particularly for business or official reasons, but also for educational, social, or recreational purposes.

b) ☐ This is used in business, in government, and law courts; it may also be the national language.

c) ☐ Used in part of a country or region mostly as a first language, usually for personal, social, or commercial reasons; sometimes for official or educational reasons.

d) ☐ The first language to be acquired at home.

e) ☐ A process involving worldwide interaction in trade, politics, recreation, education, etc.

3.2 **The following terms (1–10) all appear in Text 7-1. In groups, discuss what these terms mean, then try to match them with the definitions a–j.**

> **1** first language **2** pidgin **3** multilingual **4** lingua franca **5** vernacular
>
> **6** minority language **7** working language **8** immersion language
>
> **9** neologism **10** standardized language

a) ☐ An internationally used language of communication, e.g., English or French in Africa.

b) ☐ Referring to a language spoken by a significant number of the population (for example, a tribal language), but not the official or national language.

c) ☐ The use of three or more languages by an individual or a group of speakers.

d) ☐ A language used "comfortably" by speakers for specific purposes, e.g., for study, trade, or diplomacy.

e) ☐ A language that is systematically introduced throughout a country or region, usually by the government.

f) ☐ A language that is convenient when speakers of different languages need to communicate; usually with a limited vocabulary and grammatical structure.

g) ☐ A variety of the language that has the highest status in a nation, usually based on the speech and writing of educated native speakers of the language.

h) ☐ This usually refers to the language that a user feels most comfortable with. It is normally acquired at home or through the influence of, for example, school.

i) ☐ A newly invented word or phrase in a particular language.

j) ☐ A language spoken by relatively few people, for example, in one country or because the numbers of speakers anywhere is relatively small.

Task 4: Predicting content to help understanding

You will notice that Text 7-1 does not have a list of contents. In Ex 4.2, your instructor will show you how to devise a list of your own in the form of questions on the text.

4.1 **Reread Paragraphs A–C of Text 7-1. From reading these paragraphs, what do you think the rest of the article will be about? Write your predictions below.**

_____

_____

_____

_____

_____

_____

_____

_____

_____

4.2   **Think of questions you would like Text 7-1 to answer in relation to the assignment. Base your questions on reading Paragraphs A–C and the background information on Zambia.**

This exercise will serve as an outline of the text and help you read more efficiently.

Example: Why has English become such an influential language in a country like Zambia?

Make a list of similar questions based on your reading of Paragraphs A–C and on the background information on Zambia (page 68).
Check your answers with other students and with the instructor.

QUESTIONS ABOUT THE TEXT

Why has English become a global language?

Task 5: Selecting relevant information from the text

You should now be ready to carry out the main reading task. You have made decisions about how to read the article and what information you hope to learn from it.

5.1   **Read the rest of Text 7-1 using the following framework.**

- Begin reading the article in the way you have decided is most appropriate.

- Collect relevant information by making notes in the way you think will be most useful.

- Your instructor will give you a time limit for reading and collecting the relevant information. At the end of the time limit, form groups and compare the notes you have made so far.

- Check the information you have agreed on with the instructor.

- Continue reading and making and comparing notes until you have finished the text.

Task 6: Fulfilling your reading purpose

6.1 Using the notes you have made on Text 7-1, write two or three paragraphs in answer to the Focus task.

Unit summary

In this unit you have practiced making use of a specific text to support your ideas in a writing assignment, and learned how knowing subject-specific vocabulary will help you understand texts that you read. You have also developed all the skills you have learned so far on this reading course.

1 **Look at the topics and lists of subject-specific vocabulary. How quickly can you delete the one word or phrase that does not relate to the topic?**

a) higher education   lectures / assignment / nursery / tutoring sessions / graduation

b) computers   spreadsheet / virus / template / database / turntable

c) space exploration   satellite / archaeologist / astronaut / shuttle / orbit

d) politics   democracy / dictator / free election / divorce / coalition

e) war and peace   pension / dispute / weapons / troops / ceasefire

2 **Write three topics for which you think you have a good working vocabulary.**

_____   _____   _____

3 **Think about which strategies have helped you improve your reading skills the most. Give one piece of advice about each of the following to a student who is starting the reading course.**

a) Before reading a text, you should _____

_____

b) As you read a text, you should _____

_____

c) After reading a text, you should _____

_____

For web resources relevant to this unit, see:
www.englishforacademicstudy.com/us/student/reading/links

g Glossary

Active vocabulary
Vocabulary that you use in your day-to-day life in order to communicate effectively.

Anecdote
A short account of an incident that is amusing or interesting.

Annotate
To write comments or explanatory notes directly onto a text, e.g., in the margin.

Browsing
Reading with no particular purpose in mind, e.g., glancing over several pages and checking a few sentences or a heading, or randomly opening a book at a page to read a few lines or paragraphs.

Collocation
The way that certain words are habitually used together, e.g., *strong cheese* and *bread and butter* collocate, but not *weak cheese* or *butter and bread*.

Complex sentences
Sentences that are made up of several clauses (main and dependent clauses). They may also include long phrases or unusual syntax and/or terminology.

Critical reading
Reading in a way that involves questioning what the text says, what the writer is trying to do, and how s/he does this, e.g., whether the text is biased or prejudiced.

Extra-textual information
Information outside the text, such as the "blurb" on a book cover, diagrams, etc. that help the reader understand what the text is about.

Foreword
A section of a book or longer text that comes at the beginning and gives a short introduction to it. This introduction is often written by someone other than the author and may be in the form of a short essay.

Global summary
A short general summary (usually of one paragraph) that gives the reader a good idea of all the main ideas in a text rather than focusing on any detail. An abstract is one example of a global summary.

Global understanding
This is an understanding of the main idea(s) or argument of a text or conversation. We often skim read (or listen) for global understanding without focusing too much on detail.

Infer
To obtain or work out meaning from the text that the writer has not explicitly stated. This is sometimes called "reading between the lines" and involves the reader making use of their world knowledge.

Lexical item
An item of vocabulary such as a word or group of words that carry a single meaning, e.g., the word *sure* is one lexical item, and *absolutely convinced* is another.

Overt information
Information that is displayed in and around a text, such as headings and titles, text boxes, tables, graphs, and diagrams. Overt information, also known as displayed information, often highlights key words and ideas.

Paragraph leader
The first sentence in a written paragraph. The paragraph leader links to the ideas in the previous paragraph and may lead into the ideas in the next paragraph. The paragraph leader can sometimes also be a topic sentence.

Paraphrasing
Explaining or describing the contents or ideas of a text or part of a text, orally or in written form, using your own words and providing your own interpretation.

Prediction
The skill of using what you already know and what you want to know about a topic to guess what the text will contain. Clues such as titles, pictures, layout, and paragraph leaders can help you predict and make it less challenging to read or difficult to understand.

Previewing
Looking at text to decide how useful it is for a particular purpose. Previewing might involve looking at: the contents page, the foreword or introduction, and/or the index.

Prior knowledge
This is knowledge that you already have about something, sometimes known as *general knowledge* or *world knowledge*. If you have prior knowledge of key vocabulary or ideas in a text, e.g., from reading about it in your own language, you will generally find it easier to follow.

Purposeful reading
Having a specific reason for reading a text, e.g., reading to learn, reading for entertainment, or reading to confirm. The reading purpose will affect which reading strategy to apply, e.g., fast skimming, browsing, search reading, intensive reading, etc.

Quoting
Using the exact words of the original text for a specific purpose, orally or in writing.

Reading selectively
Selective reading involves choosing certain sections in a text to read carefully because these are the areas that you wish to understand or research in more depth. You read selectively when you have a clear purpose for reading.

Reading strategy
Something that you can actively do to help your reading, or improve your reading skills over a period of time. Typical reading strategies for academic texts include: knowing your reading purpose, picking out key words and note-taking.

Referencing
Acknowledgement of the sources of ideas and information used or mentioned in a text. References allow a reader to check those sources for accuracy or find out more information about the topic.

Scanning
Reading for specific information involves scanning. It involves finding key words or figures. For example, it is normal to scan a text to find dates, names, and specific facts.

Search reading
Looking through a text quickly to find specific *ideas* rather than *words*. It is different from scanning because you do not know the specific words you are looking for.

Skimming
Reading for the general idea or gist of a text involves skimming. It involves reading the text quickly to get the main idea of what it is about rather than focusing on every word. For example, it is normal to skim a letter or book cover to find out what it is about. It often precedes reading for more specific information.

Supporting sentences

Sentences that follow or support the main idea or topic sentence in a paragraph. Supporting sentences may give examples, explanations, or additional information about the key idea.

Text analysis

Checking the currency, authorship, purpose, accessibility, relevance, and interest value of a text.

Topic sentence

A sentence that carries the main idea of the paragraph. It often comes at the beginning or end of a paragraph, but may also appear elsewhere. It is usually followed by supporting sentences or preceded by them. There may be more than one topic sentence in a paragraph or none at all.

Word class

Words can be grouped into classes according to their function in a sentence. Word classes, also known as parts of speech, include *nouns*, *verbs*, *adjectives*, and *adverbs*.

Word family

A group of words that are closely related to each other because they share a common root or because they have related meanings, e.g., *family, familiar, familiarize, familiarization*.

Writing

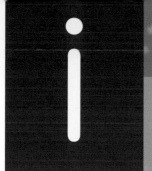

Introduction

The approach used in this Writing course combines four major aspects of writing methodology based on practical classroom experience and well-founded research. They are:

- The process approach to writing
- The development of critical thinking skills
- The microskills of writing
- The importance of genre

1. The process approach to writing

The process approach to writing has now been used widely for a number of years on writing courses throughout the world. This approach has proved itself as an effective way of improving the academic writing skills of students studying English for academic purposes. The basic concept of this approach is that good writers go through a number of processes while composing a text before they produce their final product. The main underlying principles are:

- **Writing is a recursive process.** Effective writing results from rewriting and revising at each stage of the composing process. A good writer goes back and thinks again before continuing to write. You will be asked to:

  - brainstorm ideas, i.e., think quickly to get ideas for your essay;

  - organize your ideas into a plan;

  - write your first draft;

  - revise and edit your first draft, according to peer feedback and your own developing ideas;

  - rewrite it to produce a second draft;

  - revise and edit your second draft, according to instructor feedback and your own developing ideas;

  - rewrite it to produce a third draft.

- **It helps to share and discuss the writing process with others.** Your work improves if you talk to others about your ideas and problems. Simply by talking to another student, you can clarify aspects of your work that you are not sure about. Another person will have an objective view as your reader and will be able to make useful suggestions about your writing.

  When you write, you write for an audience so you need to think about how to structure your message in order to communicate your ideas in the clearest way. It therefore helps to show your writing to others so that you can get feedback and learn how to adapt your writing to different audiences.

  During your writing course, you will have the opportunity to discuss your writing at each stage of the process.

- **A good writer is critical of her/his own work.** You should read your work carefully and consider both the strengths and weaknesses of your writing.

  a) **Self-evaluation:** To help you develop your critical ability, you will be asked to consider a series of *evaluation questions*, which you will use to evaluate your own writing.

  b) **Peer evaluation:** You will also be asked to consider a series of evaluation questions that you will use to evaluate the writing of another student. You will carry out peer evaluation by reading the student's essay, offering suggestions and commenting on it in a way that is helpful and constructive, as well as receiving comments from her/him. When reading another student's essay, you will focus on the organization of the ideas and the overall argument of the text. At this stage, this is more important than the accuracy of the language, spelling and punctuation, unless errors make the essay difficult to understand.

Your instructor will read the second draft of your essays, and will respond with comments and suggestions. Her/his feedback will focus on:

- task achievement, i.e., how well you have responded to the title of your essay;
- organization and development of ideas;
- content;
- language.

S/he will give you feedback on language problems through the use of symbols, which will indicate the type of error you have made, such as:

- Using the wrong word (WW)
- Using the wrong form of the word (WF).

Your instructor will explain this system in more detail and refer you to a key to the symbols. You will be asked to correct your language errors as well as improve other aspects of your essay; this will be your final editing work.

Although some of these approaches may be unfamiliar to you, the aim is to help you acquire skills with which you will be able to produce good written English without dependence on an instructor. This is important for your future studies.

In diagrammatic form, the process looks like this:

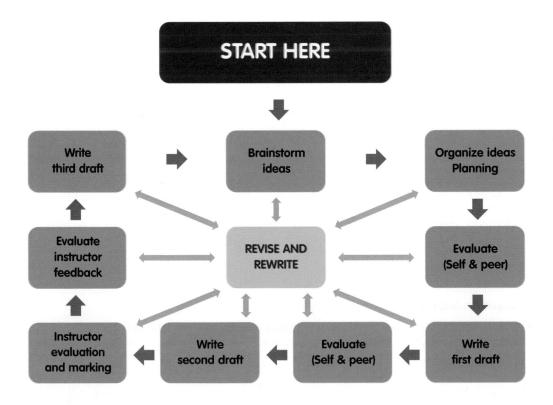

2. The development of critical thinking skills

At the advanced level necessary for your studies, academic writing should express the critical thinking and reasoning that has been used to develop the main ideas in your writing. This is a fundamental skill that is increasingly necessary for successful academic study in higher education. It could typically involve:

- assessing information in order to show how it relates to an understanding of the *truth* in a particular context;
- identifying problems;
- seeking solutions to these problems;
- evaluating the solutions;
- assessing the implications (or effect) if those solutions are applied.

Research has shown that working for a period of time on one particular topic provides a basis for developing and expressing critical thinking skills. This is one of the reasons why your writing tasks are based on specific reading texts.

Many of the tasks that you will do during the course will contribute to the development and expression of your critical thinking skills. You may discover how writing of this kind in English in higher education differs from writing in your own language.

3. The microskills of writing

EAS Writing will also deal with other important aspects of writing, such as:

- how to write an effective introduction and conclusion;
- how to communicate the main idea of a paragraph to the reader;
- how to support your main ideas with examples;
- how to express yourself in writing using more complex sentences;
- how to write accurately and fluently.

It will also help you to expand your use of language appropriate to the task.

4. The importance of genre

To a certain extent, *EAS Writing* will look at how different academic subjects require different styles of writing, i.e. genre. For example, an essay written in a science subject will typically be in a more concise style than one written in a social science subject. A variety of ways of organizing writing will therefore be analyzed and practiced. These will include essays of:

- cause and effect;
- situation, problem, solution(s), implication(s) and evaluation;
- comparison and contrast.

The course will also increase your awareness of the type of language most appropriate to express these patterns of organization. By the end of the course, you should be able to write effectively for your individual purposes, and be able to make appropriate choices when approaching a writing task. In your writing, you should be able to show clear development of a topic through good organization and language use.

5. The link between reading and writing

Research has shown that an integrated approach to the teaching of writing contributes to the development of the critical thinking skills of the student. Carson views critical thinking as:

> "the ability to transform information for their own [students'] purposes in reading and to synthesize their prior knowledge with another text in writing … Together, reading and writing facilitate the development of critical thinking." (Carson, EJ, & Leki (1993), *Reading in the Composition Classroom*, Heinle and Heinle: p.100.)

The implication of the research for teaching academic writing is that there should be an integrated skills approach that includes the specific development of critical thinking skills.

The structure of *EAS Writing* reflects this approach. Each unit has a writing topic that is based on the relevant reading text. This follows the principle that, as a student, you read an academic text for a particular purpose. One of the main purposes of the texts will be to provide relevant information to support your ideas in the written assignments. You will need to process and critically analyze that information before incorporating it within your own argument; you will, in this way, be engaging in problem-solving activities. It is important that your writing development reflects the problem-solving you will meet in your academic study.

6. Timed writing

Written examinations will be a major method of formal assessment for many of you once you start your chosen degree course. To be successful in examinations, you will need to be able to write quickly and concisely when answering a question. Writing to complete an essay within a time limit will be practiced on this course as an integral component. You will also develop your technique in quickly analyzing an examination question in order to respond to the task appropriately.

7. Some practical points

You should type your first drafts on a word processor. This is because:

- it is easier for your classmates to read;
- it is easier to make corrections and revisions to your work;
- You will be required to submit word-processed essays in your future studies.

You should use an approved university style of layout. This might be **Times New Roman font size 12** and **double spacing** for the main body of your text. However, if you have little or no experience in word processing, you should discuss with your instructor when you should begin typing your essays.

When you give your instructor the **second draft** of your essay, you will also give her/him your **plan** and your **first draft**. This will enable her/him:

- to assess the effectiveness of the process;
- to assess your response to evaluation;
- to help you further.

Similarly, when you give your instructor the **third draft** of your essay, you will also give her/him your **second draft**.

1 Academic Achievement

This unit will help you:
- think about the aims of academic study, and how to achieve them;
- learn about the different stages of the writing process;
- identify and learn how to cope with difficulties in academic writing;
- learn how to consider the knowledge and expectations of your reader;
- think about different approaches to the organization of your ideas.

Task 1: Thinking about academic success

The following questionnaire, Ex 1.1–1.14, will help you think about your views on the meaning of academic success and aspects of academic writing. You will then be able to discuss your views with the rest of the class.

1.1 **What is the aim of academic study? (Please check (✔) one or more.)**

☐ to meet intelligent people

☐ to ensure having a career or future job

☐ to discover more about theories and certain known facts

☐ to discuss philosophy

☐ to enjoy learning

☐ to enable members of society to exchange ideas that are intellectually stimulating*

☐ to develop personal growth

☐ to contribute to the social and economic development of society

☐ to pass examinations

☐ to gain a higher-level degree

☐ to improve cooperation between different members of world society

* **intellectually stimulating:** *encouraging the mind to develop further*

1.2 **How important is it for you as a student to develop the following characteristics while studying at university? (Check (✔) H for High importance, M for Medium importance, L for Low importance.)**

H	M	L	
☐	☐	☐	knowing your strengths and weaknesses
☐	☐	☐	thinking about how to further develop your abilities
☐	☐	☐	thinking about how to approach a particular task
☐	☐	☐	using a logical, reasoned approach to study
☐	☐	☐	approaching your subject in depth
☐	☐	☐	being interested in finding things out
☐	☐	☐	learning how to study
☐	☐	☐	communicating results successfully

> **Study tip**
>
> Working with information is a good way of helping you develop ideas. Doing a questionnaire is one example of this, but you can do this yourself by setting clear goals for reading text, e.g., having several clear questions you would like to answer.

Reading & Writing

1.3 **What is academic writing? (Please check (✔) one or more.)**

- [ ] a mechanical exercise
- [ ] groups of grammatically correct sentences
- [ ] the clear expression of ideas, knowledge and information
- [ ] a form of self-expression
- [ ] a way of exploring, addressing and expressing academic issues
- [ ] a way of communicating results or information

1.4 **To write well academically, how important are the following? (Check (✔) H for High importance, M for Medium importance, L for Low importance.)**

H M L

- [ ] [ ] [ ] reading a lot
- [ ] [ ] [ ] studying grammar
- [ ] [ ] [ ] studying vocabulary
- [ ] [ ] [ ] imitating other writers
- [ ] [ ] [ ] writing a lot
- [ ] [ ] [ ] inviting others to comment on your writing
- [ ] [ ] [ ] going back and thinking again about what you have written
- [ ] [ ] [ ] rewriting repeatedly until you are satisfied
- [ ] [ ] [ ] understanding the process of writing
- [ ] [ ] [ ] meeting the needs of your reader

1.5 **How important do you think the following are when writing academic texts? (Check (✔) H for High importance, M for Medium importance, L for Low importance.)**

H M L

- [ ] [ ] [ ] grammatical correctness
- [ ] [ ] [ ] spelling and punctuation (using periods, commas, etc.)
- [ ] [ ] [ ] an appropriate style
- [ ] [ ] [ ] overall organization
- [ ] [ ] [ ] vocabulary
- [ ] [ ] [ ] good ideas
- [ ] [ ] [ ] good use of sources (appropriate citation, bibliography)
- [ ] [ ] [ ] relevance of subject content
- [ ] [ ] [ ] response to the task

1.6 **In which of the following ways can you support your ideas when writing academic texts?**

- [ ] using personal anecdotes*
- [ ] using facts
- [ ] using statistics

- [ ] using examples
- [ ] using the news
- [ ] using information from books, articles, reports, the Internet
- [ ] using analogies**
- [ ] using the views and attitudes of others
- [ ] using research data

* anecdote: *a short, often amusing account of something that has happened*

** analogy: *to make or draw an analogy between two things is to show they are alike in some way*

1.7 **Which of the following contribute to successful academic writing?**

- [ ] presenting information clearly and precisely
- [ ] analyzing questions and issues clearly and precisely
- [ ] distinguishing between relevant and irrelevant material
- [ ] recognizing key assumptions*
- [ ] identifying competing points of view
- [ ] demonstrating excellent reasoning and problem-solving abilities
- [ ] adopting a critical stance**
- [ ] understanding the context for which you are writing

* assumption: *if you make an assumption that something is true, you accept it is true without any real proof or evidence*

** critical stance: *to take a critical stance is to have a strong viewpoint on something after examining and judging it carefully*

1.8 **When persuading your professor or other members of your academic community that your argument is valid, how important are the following? (Check (✔) H for High importance, M for Medium importance, L for Low importance.)**

H	M	L	
[ ]	[ ]	[ ]	analyzing questions
[ ]	[ ]	[ ]	stating facts
[ ]	[ ]	[ ]	reasoning your argument logically from facts
[ ]	[ ]	[ ]	explaining key terms
[ ]	[ ]	[ ]	using language appropriate to a particular subject area
[ ]	[ ]	[ ]	using other points of view to strengthen your argument or research
[ ]	[ ]	[ ]	demonstrating the weaknesses of other people's arguments
[ ]	[ ]	[ ]	acknowledging the limitations of your own argument or research
[ ]	[ ]	[ ]	supporting your argument with examples
[ ]	[ ]	[ ]	frequently summarizing your argument
[ ]	[ ]	[ ]	referring to well-argued conclusions

Reading & Writing

1.9 Should you always think of academic writing as communicating with another person? Why/Why not?

1.10 What do you do, or what do you concentrate on, when you are given a writing task:

a) while you are still writing your first draft?

b) when you have finished your first draft?

c) before you hand in your final draft?

1.11 What type of academic writing have you done in the past?

1.12 What difficulties do you have with writing in English or in your own language?

1.13 **What do you do when you have difficulties?**

_____

_____

_____

_____

1.14 **Do you enjoy academic writing? Why/Why not?**

_____

_____

_____

_____

When you have finished the questionnaire, compare your answers with those of other people in your group. Discuss your answers, and keep notes of the discussion. Do you find that you all have very similar views and experiences? Or are your views and experiences very different? Are there any general trends among students in the group?

Material adapted from White, R.V. (1994). *Writing English for academic study series* **and Richards, R. (2001).** *Presenting critical thinking as a study strategy for UK higher education.*

Text 1 | Academic achievement (pp. 157–161)

You will have an opportunity to read these extracts from articles in the *Scientific American* during this stage. This will help you identify information that is relevant to the title of your essay.

Task 2: Microskills: Planning

The essay that you will prepare in this unit is on the following topic:

> What are the aims of academic study and how can they be achieved?

Before you begin writing, you should spend some time:

- thinking about exactly what the question is asking you to write about;
- generating ideas about the topic; this is called *brainstorming*;
- organizing your ideas into a plan.

As part of this preparation, you should read Texts 1-1, 1-2, and 1-3 to identify relevant information. You might also find that some of the ideas generated by the questionnaire and discussion in Task 1 will help you.

2.1 Discuss what you think the key words are in the essay question:

a) with a partner;

b) with the whole group and your instructor.

2.2 Spend five minutes writing down all the ideas you can think of that are relevant to the essay topic. Write notes, not complete sentences, so that your ideas flow. The order of your ideas is not important at this stage.

2.3 Discuss the ideas you have written in Ex 2.2:

a) with a partner;

b) with the whole group and your instructor.

2.4 Decide which of your ideas you are going to use in your essay.

a) To help you, ask yourself these questions about your readers:
  - What knowledge about academic study do they already have?
  - What do you think they are interested in reading about in your essay?

b) When you have decided which ideas you are going to include, organize them into a logical order in a plan. You may want to develop some of the ideas further and you may want to add a new idea.
  - Group together ideas that seem to belong to the same paragraph.
  - Think carefully about the order in which you will arrange the paragraphs.

2.5 Discuss your plan with your partner. When you look at your partner's plan, ask yourself:

- What is the overall idea in the essay?
- Does the plan follow a logical sequence of ideas?
- Are the ideas grouped effectively into paragraphs?
- Is the main idea clear in each paragraph?
- How many paragraphs will the essay contain?

If the answers to these questions are not clear from looking at your partner's plan, ask her/him to explain. Perhaps the plan needs to be changed or developed more.

Note: Remember your plan is your guide; when you think more and start writing, you may need to change it, so keep evaluating it.

2.6 Think about your partner's comments on your plan and try to improve it.

2.7 Write the first draft of your essay. At this stage, you should try to write between 400 and 600 words.

2.8 **When you have finished your first draft, find another student who has also finished and exchange drafts.**

a) Read your partner's draft carefully. Respond to the questions on the Peer Evaluation Sheet for Unit 1 on page 141 of this book.

b) When commenting on your partner's draft, remember that *constructive criticism* is more helpful when giving advice. The phrases below for making polite suggestions should help you to express your comments in a constructive manner.

Giving Peer Feedback
PHRASES FOR MAKING POLITE SUGGESTIONS

- It might be a good idea if you …
- It might be a good idea to …
- I agree with you, but you could …
- Right, but you could …
- This is/That's good, but you could …
- My advice would be to …
- Do you think a better approach might be to …?
- Why don't you …?
- How about this?
- Perhaps you could …
- Maybe it would be better to …
- I think it would be better if you …
- Can I/May I make another suggestion?
- I would recommend that you …
- Have you thought about (verb + *ing*) …?
- What about …?

Remember: Peer feedback should be supportive and helpful—provide *constructive criticism*.

Task 3: Microskills: Introductions

3.1 **Quickly write down what you think are the important points to include in an introduction to an academic essay.**

3.2 **Discuss your ideas and explain why you have chosen these points:**

a) with a partner;

b) with the rest of the class.

Study tip

EAS Writing contains suggestions for individual work as well as pair, group, and class discussion. Make full use of this varied interaction to develop your ideas.

3.3 **Answer the following questions:**

a) What function or purpose does the introduction of an essay have?

_____

_____

_____

_____

_____

_____

_____

b) What should an introduction contain?

_____

_____

_____

_____

_____

_____

_____

_____

_____

3.4 **Look at the following sentences from an introduction to an essay on The problems of population growth.**

a) Decide which would be the most logical order of these sentences:

❶

This growth has created many problems, especially in the capital cities.

❷

This essay will discuss the situation that has led to the development of these problems and describe some of them.

❸

The population of the world has been growing rapidly over the last thirty years.

❹

It will then suggest some possible solutions to the problems and evaluate their viability.

❺

The problems include housing, pollution, unemployment, and food and water shortages.

b) Compare what you think with another student and also say why you decided on the order you chose.

c) Together with your partner, try to identify an obvious pattern to the introduction and decide what the function of each sentence is.

3.5 **Read carefully the following five introductions for an essay entitled Academic success in one's own culture and try to evaluate their strengths and weaknesses.**

❶

There are different programs for education in different countries. Every country has a special education system that is adapted to each country. In Iran, the education system is organized from primary school to university. This essay is about the academic success in Iran.

❷

Academic success is one of the most important goals of many students in Thailand. There are some relevant factors to obtain this goal. In Thailand, if you can enter college, it means that you succeed in your life. Every year, most final-year students try to enter college; however, some students prefer to study in small colleges. This essay will describe some factors that are closely related to academic success in Thailand.

❸

Everybody wishes to achieve success in society. "Success" in Chinese society is not only for one's own honor, but also the whole family's. Furthermore, for most Chinese students, in the first stage, our academic success might be that required to gain a good score and enter a higher school to study. In the second stage, it might be that needed for a student to find a good job or contribute to specific academic fields. It could be called "academic success." In addition, our education system and concept of traditional culture always affects our students' success. Therefore, this essay will describe academic success in Taiwan and indicate the related factors.

④ Education is one of the basic factors contributing to the development of a society. The educated or literate people could realize their potential livelihood. By extending education in Africa, the people may improve their cultural attitudes. This essay will describe the education system in Africa.

⑤ What is academic success in our country? Many factors to describe it can be found. As this topic mentioned, its importance depends on the following: intelligence, teaching methods, the policy of the government, the system of education, support system, and facilities. At first, I would like to define the meaning, before answering this question. When this question—what kind of fact is regarded as academic success in Japan—is asked, most Japanese will answer that it is to graduate from a high-grade university. There is a good reason to say so. In Japanese society, there is the fact that an academic career decides a students' future life. If they obtain a high grade in their school career, probably it will mean success in their future. After graduating, most of them will be able to enter a prestigious company. Generally, this is a useful occupation and its conditions are good. Therefore, many people take much time to prepare for passing school exams. Some children have to study hard before they attain the school age. Under these circumstances, it seems that they forget the meaning of studying subjects. This essay mentions motivation to study and tries to clear up the meaning of academic success in our culture.

Edited extracts from authentic student material

3.6 **Imagine you are writing an essay on the following three topics. Write a suitable introduction for each one of them. (Note that you are not going to write the whole essay.)**

a) The education system in one's own country.

b) Traveling broadens the mind. Discuss.

c) The rapid development of electronic communications may mean that people will have fewer social skills. Discuss.

3.7 **When you write the second draft of your essay *What are the aims of academic study and how can they be achieved?* make appropriate changes to the introduction, and other parts, according to your peer feedback session.**

Unit summary

In this unit you have reflected on your attitudes and approach to academic writing skills. You have thought about the different stages of the writing process and practiced planning, writing a first draft, and giving peer feedback. You have also looked at how to write effective introductions to your essays.

1   **Match the words and phrases in the box to their definitions below. They are all procedures and techniques that form part of the writing process.**

> drafting   brainstorming   peer feedback   organizing ideas   adopting a critical stance

a)   Generating and noting down initial ideas about a topic without ordering them

b)   Putting ideas together in a logical sequence

c)   Deciding on and expressing your viewpoint after examining and judging possible opinions

d)   The process of writing and putting your essay together. Most essays will have two or more drafts and will be revised and edited after each draft.

e)   Comments on your essay from other students

2   **Complete the sentences below on writing an academic text using some of the words from Ex 1.**

a)   When you are given a writing task, it is important to start by

_____

_____

b)   When you write the first draft you should

_____

_____

c)   Before you hand in your final draft

_____

_____

_____

3   **After working on this unit, write down ways in your notebook of how you improved your knowledge of academic writing.**

> For web resources relevant to this unit, see:
> **www.englishforacademicstudy.com/us/student/writing/links**

2 Early Human Development

This unit will help you:
- make decisions about what the essay title is asking you to write about;
- consider the most appropriate way to organize your ideas;
- decide what information in a text is useful to support your ideas;
- practice writing paragraph leaders.

Text 2   Early human development (pp. 162–165)

You will have an opportunity to read three extracts from *Hilgard's introduction to psychology* during this stage. This will help you prepare your essay.

Task 1: Microskills: Organizing your ideas

This unit will prepare you to write the following essay:

> Nurture strongly influences early human development. Discuss.

Some words in essay titles are more important than others, because they contain the main ideas of the topic. These words can be called key words, because they generate the main ideas that you need to include in your essay and, to a certain extent, control the content of your essay.

1.1   Study the essay title for this unit.
- Which are the *key* words in the essay title for this unit?
- Why do you think they are the *key* words?

1.2   Discuss your ideas with another student.

1.3   Spend five minutes writing down all the ideas you can think of that may be relevant to this essay.
Remember, you do not need to write complete sentences.

_____

_____

_____

_____

_____

_____

1.4 Discuss your ideas with two other students. Together, decide which ideas are particularly relevant to the topic and the best ones to use in your essay.

1.5 Which of the following do you think the essay is asking you to do?

a) Explain all the influences on early human development to your reader.

b) Persuade your reader that one kind of influence is the strongest.

c) Write a historical description of all theories concerning early human development.

d) Explain to your reader that research has shown there are different influences on early human development, and persuade her/him that one of these influences is stronger than the others.

Study tip

It is essential that you understand what the essay title wants you to do. The more time you spend on this at the beginning, the more time you will save when you write your essay. You will have more work on this in Unit 3.

1.6 Discuss your choice and explain why you made that choice:

a) with one or two other students;

b) with the rest of the class.

1.7 What would be an appropriate way to organize your ideas for this type of essay? Why? Discuss possible ways to organize your ideas with one or two other students.

1.8 Read the three extracts—Texts 2-1, 2-2, and 2-3. What ideas and information from the texts could help you to develop your own ideas and provide *academic evidence* to support your argument?

1.9 Discuss your decisions with a partner.

1.10 Organize your ideas into a logical order in a plan that clearly shows the structure of your essay. Remember that time spent planning now can save you time later, when you are actually writing.

Study tip

Writing a clear plan will save you time later.

- Group together ideas that seem to belong to the same paragraph.

- Give enough information to show how you will support your ideas.

- Think carefully about the order in which you will arrange the paragraphs.

1.11 Read another student's plan and answer the following questions about it:

- What is the overall idea in the essay?

- Is it obvious from the section on the introduction what the writer's thesis is?

- Does the plan follow a logical sequence of ideas?

- Are the ideas grouped effectively into paragraphs?

- Is the main idea clear in each paragraph?

- How many paragraphs will the essay contain?

If the answers to these questions are not clear from looking at your partner's plan, ask her/him to explain. Perhaps the plan needs to be changed or developed further.

1.12 Consider your partner's comments on your plan and try to improve it.

1.13 Write the first draft of your essay, aiming to write between 400 and 600 words.

1.14 When you have finished your first draft, find another student who has also finished and exchange drafts.

a) Read your partner's draft carefully.

b) Respond to the questions on the Peer Evaluation Sheet for Unit 2 on page 142 of this book.

Task 2: Microskills: Paragraph leaders

2.1 Look at the following sentences from the text *Early human development* again and underline the key ideas.

a) Motor development after birth also illustrates the interaction between genetically programmed maturation and environmental influence. (paragraph F, page 163)

b) Although early studies suggested that the answer was no (McGraw, 1935/1975; Dennis & Dennis, 1940; Gesell & Thompson, 1929), more recent studies indicate that practice or extra stimulation can accelerate the appearance of motor behaviors to some extent. (paragraph G, page 163)

c) The development of speech provides another example of the interaction between genetically determined characteristics and experience. (paragraph H, page 163)

> **Study tip**
>
> When you are writing, try to think of your audience and how they will make sense of your ideas. Using clear paragraph leaders will help the reader follow more easily.

2.2 Discuss your ideas and decide what information you might expect to follow each of the above sentences:

a) with another student;

b) with the whole class.

2.3 These sentences are the first ones in paragraphs F, G and H. Look at these three paragraphs in the text.

a) See if you were right about what information might follow the sentences.

b) Decide what function these sentences have within the paragraphs.

c) Discuss your ideas with another student.

2.4 Now read the following information on paragraph leaders and discuss how it ties in with what you have done in Ex 2.1–2.3.

The first sentence in a paragraph can be called a paragraph leader. One key function of paragraph leaders is often to anticipate the ideas that follow. This type of paragraph leader (also called a topic sentence) helps the reader to understand the focus and direction of the paragraph.

2.5 Imagine you are going to write a paragraph on *The use of e-mail in companies.* Which of the following sentences would make a suitable paragraph leader?

a) E-mail is useful in the office.

b) One of the most useful functions of e-mail is to communicate efficiently with colleagues abroad.

c) There are many uses made of e-mail in the office environment; each of these has attached to it both advantages and disadvantages.

2.6 Discuss your answer with another student and give reasons for your choice.

2.7 Imagine you are going to write a paragraph on the benefits for international students of studying in an American university. Which of the following sentences would make a suitable paragraph leader?

a) Studying in an American university is useful for many reasons.

b) Studying in an American university provides students with a number of benefits.

c) International students prefer to study in the US.

2.8 Discuss your answer with another student and give reasons for your choice.

2.9 The paragraph leaders of the following paragraphs have been removed. Read the paragraphs and write a suitable paragraph leader for each one.

Since English has become the most widely used international language in most fields, many employers require their employees to have a high level of English. It is especially useful for those in academic posts, as so many academic papers are published in English. Those working in financial markets also need English in order to be able to talk to their English-speaking clients and to work effectively in the international market. Other fields for which it is useful to know English include business, commerce, and diplomacy. Thus, one of the advantages of being competent in the English language is that there is a wider range of career opportunities.

The first option of building more roads needs to be examined very carefully, as one of the possible effects of further construction is an increase in the volume of traffic, which happened when the freeway around the city was built. The second option, that of limiting the number of cars on the road at one time, will not meet with the approval of the general public. The third option, that of providing a more extensive, more efficient and cheaper transport system, seems to be the most viable one. It would encourage people to leave their cars at home, as they would benefit more from using public transport. So the third option should be examined in more detail in order to establish a new system.

Edited extracts from authentic student material

2.10 Make appropriate changes to your essay for Unit 2, considering the work on paragraph leaders that you have developed in Task 2.

Unit summary

In this unit you have worked on developing skills necessary for organizing your ideas. You have also looked at using *paragraph leaders* to indicate the topic of the paragraph and link it to previous and subsequent ideas.

1   **Think about the activities you have worked on in this unit and the skills they have practiced. Complete the following table with the appropriate activity number:**

Skill	Task / Activity
Deciding what the essay is asking you to write about	
Deciding the most appropriate way of organizing your ideas	
Deciding what information in a text is useful to support your ideas	
Incorporating that information in your writing	
Effectively introducing your reader to the main idea in each paragraph	

2   **Complete the list of activities below with words from the box.**

> develop   discuss   group   plan   first draft   key words   relevant
>
> academic evidence   related ideas   paragraph leader   general statements

Organizing your ideas for an academic essay

Planning

a)   Identify the _____ in the essay title.

b)   Quickly write down all the ideas you can think of that may be _____ to the topic.

c)   _____ what the essay is asking for with other students.

d)   Read texts on the topic to help _____ your own ideas and provide _____ for your opinions

Drafting

e)   _____ your ideas so that _____ are all in the same paragraph.

f)   Introduce the topic with _____ and gradually become more specific.

g)   Read and comment on another student's _____ or _____.

h)   Make sure that you include a clear _____ at the start of each paragraph.

For web resources relevant to this unit, see:
www.englishforacademicstudy.com/us/student/writing/links

3b Telemedicine

This unit will help you:
- understand the differences between writing an essay in an exam and writing a course assignment;
- learn how to analyze the essay question quickly;
- make decisions about the most appropriate way to organize your ideas;
- complete an essay within a time limit.

Task 1: Microskills: Writing in exams

Writing essays under exam conditions is an important aspect of academic study. This unit will help you understand the differences between writing an essay in an exam and writing a class assignment.

Study tip

This unit contains crucial information that will help you when writing in exam questions. Make sure you refer back to the Key writing skills on pages 100 and 102 for revision purposes.

1.1 **Think about your experience of writing an essay in an examination. Then answer the following questions.**

a) What is the first thing that you do?

b) What is the second thing that you do?

c) What are the next stages that you go through?

1.2 **Discuss your ideas with another student.**

1.3 **Write down three differences between writing in an exam and writing a class assignment.**

1.4 **Discuss your ideas with your partner.**

1.5 Check (✔) the appropriate boxes in the following table to show which stages in the process of writing academic essays apply to exams, and which apply to course assignments.

Stage in the process	Writing essays in exams	Course assignments
Analyzing the title		
Brainstorming ideas		
Organizing your ideas/plan		
Self-evaluation		
Peer evaluation		
Writing a first draft		
Self-evaluation		
Peer evaluation		
Revising your draft		
Writing a second draft		
Professor evaluation/feedback		
Evaluation of professor feedback		
Revising your second draft		
Writing a third draft		
Writing a final draft		

1.6 **Discuss your views with your partner.**

Key writing skills: As you will have seen, writing essays in exams is similar to writing course assignments in a number of ways, but different in other ways. The main difference is the time constraint, which means that you do not have time to completely revise your essay in a second draft. However, you should always leave five or ten minutes at the end of the exam to check your work for spelling and grammar mistakes, and also for adding any information you may wish to include to improve your answer. Despite the time constraint, it is still important that you spend time:

- **analyzing** the title for the key words and to see what the essay is asking you to do (two or three minutes should be enough). The words have been chosen very carefully by the examiners to get the appropriate answer;
- **brainstorming** your ideas (three minutes should be enough);
- **organizing** your ideas into a plan (five minutes should be enough).

Remember: As you do not have time to write more than one draft of your essay, it is important to have a good plan that can guide you in the structure and direction of your argument.

1.7 **The essay questions on the next page come from genuine past exams. Read the questions and decide what they are asking you to do. For example, do you have to describe a process or compare two viewpoints?**

Food science

1 a) What properties of microorganisms lead to their being major causes of food spoilage? (7 marks)

b) Explain what you mean by food spoilage and describe the mechanisms by which microbes cause food spoilage. (7 marks)

b) How, in practice, may microbial food spoilage be reduced or prevented? (6 marks)

Animals in agriculture

2 Discuss reasons why keeping livestock may be particularly important to the welfare of the poorest people of developing countries.

3 Define what is meant by "breed" in domestic animals. Genetic change in a population may be achieved by breed substitution, crossbreeding, and within breed selection. Define these terms, giving examples.

4 Compare and contrast the characteristics of typical feed resources for ruminant and non-ruminant livestock. Bearing in mind these different feed resources, why does current thinking predict a major expansion for non-ruminant animals in the next 20 years?

Politics of the international political economy

5 "Free trade is essential for international economic growth." Discuss.

6 "International aid is the key to global development." Discuss.

7 Does the prevailing structure of north–south relations prevent the effective development of the less developed countries?

Advanced software engineering

8 a) Software Quality Systems usually contain quality control, quality assurance and quality management components. Give a brief explanation of the need for these three components and examples of their usage. (10 points)

b) Discuss the role and importance of software inspection for quality systems. (5 points)

c) Explain how "quality standards" relate to Software Quality Systems. (10 points)

Horticulture

9 What techniques can be used to minimize the wastage of irrigation water in horticultural production?

Animal sciences

10 Write an essay entitled: "Ecological implications of global warming."

Environmental hydrogeology

11 Describe the problems that subsurface drainage from impermeable surfaces may pose to groundwater, and discuss the advantages and disadvantages of using such drainage.

1.8 **Discuss your ideas with another student.**

Text 3b | Telemedicine comes home (pp. 172–174)

You will have an opportunity to read the article on telemedicine in Text 3b to stimulate your thoughts for the writing topic.

Task 2: Writing your essay

2.1 **Study the following essay title.**

a) What are the key ideas?

b) What is the question asking you to do?

> As technology continues to improve, the range of potential uses of telemedicine will increase. Telemedicine will offer more beneficial applications in preventing disease than in curing disease. Discuss.

2.2 **Discuss your ideas with your partner.**

2.3 **Brainstorm your ideas on this topic. To stimulate your thoughts further on this topic, read the article from *The Economist* entitled *Telemedicine comes home* (Text 3b).**

2.4 **Organize your ideas into a plan.**

2.5 **Write your essay. You should now feel able to write at least 600 words.**

Study tip

Use your time efficiently during exams, and make sure you leave time to check your work.

Key writing skills:

- **Read** the question very carefully. **Underline** key terminology; this will help you understand the type of answer required.

- **Brainstorm** the topic; quickly write down every idea you have that could be relevant to the question.

- **Read** the question again to check that you haven't forgotten anything. **Evaluate** your ideas, crossing out irrelevant ones.

- **Organize** relevant ideas in a plan.

- **Write** your answer, starting with a very brief introduction that contains **a thesis statement that responds to the question and anticipates the main ideas of your answer.**

- **Divide** your essay into paragraphs, each beginning with an appropriate paragraph leader that is linked to the main idea in your paragraph.

- **Support** your leading sentences with details and examples.

- **Use** linking words to guide the reader through the essay.

- **Leave** five to ten minutes at the end to reread your essay to check the clarity of your ideas, and your spelling and language.

Task 3: Key words used in exam questions

In Ex 1.7, you analyzed a number of essay questions to find out exactly what they wanted you to do. One crucial aspect of understanding essay questions is the meaning of key words used in them. Match the following words in the two boxes (a–j and k–t) to their definitions (1–10 and 11–20), and make sure you have a thorough understanding of them.

a	account	1		give an explanation of something in detail (what it is like, how it works, etc.)
b	analyze	2		a) give an _____ of—describe b) _____ for—give the reasons for
c	apply (to)	3		describe and say what you think about something
d	comment (on)	4		write in detail about all the different aspects of an issue or statement, including reasons for a particular viewpoint (give your own viewpoint or evidence that you have thought about a topic)
e	compare	5		give your views on something, say what you think about something; it is often used with a quotation, with which you should agree or disagree
f	consider	6		consider very carefully/examine to find out what something consists of
g	contrast	7		put something to use, show how something (e.g., a theory, certain findings, data, research results) can be used in a particular situation
h	define	8		describe the main aspects of two or more things to show their differences
i	describe	9		describe the main aspects of two or more things to show their similarities
j	discuss	10		give an explanation of the meaning of a term

k	evaluate	11		give the main ideas
l	explain	12		recognize items that belong to a particular group/category
m	identify	13		show the connection between two or more things
n	illustrate	14		give evidence to strengthen your point
o	outline	15		write about something in detail from the point of view of its strengths and weaknesses, advantages and disadvantages, and importance
p	prove	16		say clearly
q	relate	17		write the main points of a topic
r	summarize	18		include many examples
s	support	19		show that something is true
t	state	20		write to express the issue or idea clearly; a) explain why—give the reason for, cause of something, b) explain how—describe (a process) clearly

Adapted from Wallace, M.J. (1980). *Study Skills in English.* Cambridge: C.U.P. and Braine, G. & May, C. (1996). *Writing from Sources.* Mountain View, CA: Mayfield.

Unit summary

In this unit you have practiced using essay writing skills (such as analyzing questions and organizing ideas) within a time limit.

1   **Think about the questions below and write brief answers.**

a) How is the process of writing in exams similar to that of writing extended course assignments?

_____

b) If you have no time to write a second draft of your essay, what can you do instead?

_____

c) What do you need to look for and highlight when you read the essay title?

_____

d) What should you include in your introduction?

_____

e) What do you need to check for before handing in your work?

_____

2   **Complete the essay titles with verbs from the unit. There may be several possibilities for each title.**

a) It has been claimed that microwave radiation from mobile phones "may cause serious diseases and disturbances in the physiology" (Carlo, 2002). _____ this statement and _____ the evidence that supports or contradicts it.

b) Are mobile phones essential or dangerous? _____ the arguments for and against the use of mobile phones.

c) Wireless networking and Bluetooth: _____ the characteristics of each and _____ their performance and functions.

3   **Choose three or four more verbs from Ex 2.5 and 3.1 and write more essay titles in your notebook using them.**

For web resources relevant to this unit, see:
www.englishforacademicstudy.com/us/student/writing/links

Statistics without Tears

This unit will help you:
- make decisions about what the essay title is asking you to do, and organize your ideas;
- consider what Information in a text is useful to support your ideas, and how to incorporate that in your own writing;
- learn how to end a paragraph with an effective concluding sentence;
- practice effectively ending an essay with a conclusion.

Text 4 — Statistics without tears (pp. 175–183)

You will have the opportunity to read a variety of extracts from the book *Statistics without tears* during this stage. These extracts will provide you with useful background information.

Task 1: Microskills: Organizing your ideas

The essay that you will prepare in this unit is on the following topic:

> *Statistics should be interpreted with caution as they can be misleading; they can both lie and tell the truth. Discuss.*

To support your ideas, you should make particular reference to the use of statistics in your own subject area as well as in other areas of life.

1.1 What are the key ideas in the essay title?

1.2 Discuss your views with another student.

1.3 In five minutes, make notes on any ideas you have that are relevant to this essay and what it is asking you to do.

Study tip

Organization of ideas is a key component of good essay writing. The tasks you carry out in Unit 4 build on the work you did in Unit 2.

1.4 Discuss your ideas with one or two other students.

1.5 What would be an appropriate way of organizing your ideas for this essay? Be prepared to discuss your reasons:

a) with another student;

b) with the rest of the class.

1.6 Read Texts 4-1, 4-2, and 4-3 in order to develop further ideas for your essay.

1.7 Read the article below on crime in the UK, and decide on its main focus.

Surge in violence, or just a quirk?

Public confidence in the national crime statistics has never been high. Opinion polls repeatedly tell us that the public think crime has been rising remorselessly despite the fact that on the best measure that we have available—the British
5 Crime Survey—it has fallen by more than a third since 1995. Indeed, when Charles Clarke was home secretary he thought this lack of public trust had got so bad that it was no longer possible to have a grown-up debate about alternative criminal justice policies.

10 The fiasco over the Home Office publication of the latest quarterly crime figures does nothing to repair that damage. On the face of it there was a good set of figures to report. Overall, on both the BCS and police recorded crime figures the headline crime rate is down by 6% in the twelve months to June 2008, dispelling fears that the economic downturn had already sent the crime rate soaring.

15 Even on violence, the overall picture is encouraging. The murder rate is down by 10%, gun crime by 6% and the 237,000 offenses categorized as violence against the person recorded by the police between April and June this year is down 7% on the previous year.

Yet this reassuring picture was punctured by the disclosure that the number of offenses recorded and categorized by the police as the "most serious violence against the person"
20 between April and June this year rose by 22%.

The Home Office, unusually for the quarterly crime figures, held a journalists' briefing to explain this apparently alarming figure in the violent crime sub-category. So is this a statistical quirk or does it represent a real surge in the most violent crimes in England and Wales and a consistent under-recording of the most serious violent crime by the police?

25 Professor Paul Wiles, the Home Office's director of research and statistics, explained that the extent of the problem became clear only after an agreed clarification of the counting rules was issued to police forces in April.

This said that a case where there was clear evidence of intent to commit grievous bodily harm should be classified as a 'most serious violent offense' regardless of whether the victim had
30 been injured.

cont'd

Surge in violence, or just a quirk? (cont'd)

Wiles cited the example of a nightclub fight in which a woman smashes a bottle on a nightclub table and then lunges at her victim, but only succeeds in cutting her nose and giving her a nosebleed.

35 It now transpires that many, if not all, of the 43 police forces in England and Wales had been recording such incidents in the alternative—and less serious—category of "other violence against the person with and without injury".

After the clarification was issued, 13 police forces reported that the number of GBH [grievous bodily harm] with intent cases they were reporting had almost doubled. The Home 40 Office asked them to do a recount and they estimated that two-thirds of the 22% rise in this category of violent crime was down to the change in interpretation of the counting rules.

The actual increase in more serious violent offenses was only 5%—amounting to about 200 assaults out of a total of 237,000 violent crimes. This view was endorsed by the Association of Chief Police Officers.

45 The net result of this recategorization is a full-scale row about what appears at first sight to be a headline surge in serious violent crime, so undermining, once again, any more balanced picture of the falling crime rate in England and Wales.

Alan Travis. Copyright Guardian News & Media Ltd 2008.

See Appendix 1 on page 146 for additional questions and a glossary to accompany this text.

1.8 **In pairs or groups, discuss in what situations, and by whom, statistics are *manipulated*, so that the complete truth is hidden.**

1.9 **Now consider who produces statistics and why they produce them. Discuss your ideas with a partner.**
As you have seen, crime is one area in which statistics are used to present a particular situation. They may, or may not, represent the true situation.

1.10 **Look at the chart on page 108 and write notes to answer the following questions:**

a) What does the chart show?

_____

b) What conclusions could you draw about the UK from these statistics?

_____

c) Who produced these statistics?

_____

d) Where do they obtain their information?

_____

e) Who might benefit from these statistics?

_____

f) Why and how might they benefit?

_____

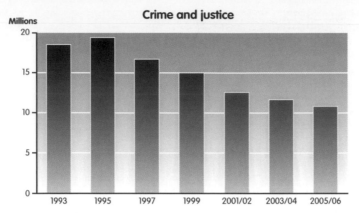

Crime and justice

British Crime Survey offenses, England and Wales

Source: UK Statistics Authority website: www.statisticsauthority.gov.uk or www.statistics.gov.uk

1.11 Discuss your ideas with one or two other students.

1.12 Can you think of situations in your own subject area when statistics on the same subject are reported, but can suggest different viewpoints? Exchange your ideas with two other students.

Task 2: Writing your essay

2.1 Use the ideas you have generated in Task 1 to write a logical plan that clearly shows the structure of the essay you are going to write.

2.2 Read another student's plan and answer the following questions about her/his plan:

a) What is the overall idea in the essay?

b) Is it obvious from the section on the Introduction what the writer's thesis is?

c) Does the plan follow a logical sequence of ideas?

d) Are the ideas grouped effectively into paragraphs?

e) Is the main idea clear in each paragraph?

f) How many paragraphs will the essay contain?

If the answers to these questions are not clear from looking at your partner's plan, ask her/him to explain. Perhaps the plan needs to be changed or developed more.

2.3 Consider your partner's comments on your plan and try to improve it.

2.4 Write the first draft of your essay.

2.5 When you have finished your first draft, find another student who has finished and exchange drafts.

a) Read your partner's draft carefully.

b) Respond to the questions on the Peer Evaluation Sheet for Unit 4 on page 143 of this book.

Task 3: Microskills: Concluding sentences

3.1 Read the following paragraphs. What function does the final sentence in each paragraph have?

❶

The rapidity or velocity of migration can be assessed in two ways. First, the movement of people across regions in given time periods can be considered, assessing the length of time a mass migration takes from its inception to its conclusion. Second, velocity in individual terms can be considered—the amount of time it takes a migrant to get from his or her original locale to a new host country. Clearly, changes in transportation technology have made a major difference in this respect. (p. 284)

❷

Trade in the sense of the exchange of goods and services between people over distance has a long history. Great trading empires have arisen periodically ever since regular long-distance travel became possible. But international trade, the exchange of goods and services between nations, by definition only emerged with the establishment of the nation state. Trade has been entwined with the rise of the modern state and its fortunes: states required revenues, above all to wage military campaigns, and trade offered an obvious source of funds. Identifying historical patterns of trade globalization is the primary objective of this chapter, and this entails deploying the analytical framework developed in the introduction. (p. 149)

❸

Rapid demographic growth is a key factor in explaining the increasing immiseration of sub-Saharan Africa and processes of desertification and soil decline. This has contributed to the growing economic problems of the region and its mounting international debts. Thus environmental problems in single African states have spilt over into the international politics of banking. The resolution of these international issues has involved political contests and struggles between Western governments and their financial sectors. In the future, the demographic and environmental squeeze on the South may contribute towards political instability and outward migration, both of which will affect a widening pool of other nations, internationally and domestically. (p. 379)

❹

In the last twenty years, a series of technological and political changes have transformed the televisual landscape and have contributed to the globalization of television as a medium and as an industry. First and foremost,

Con't

the number of countries with broadcasting systems and number of televisions available on which to watch their output has steadily risen. From its Western core, television has spread in the postwar years across Eastern Europe and the Soviet Union, into Latin America, Asia, and Africa. Second, first within the West, but later in other areas as well, the number of terrestrial channels has steadily climbed. In part, this has been because governments have been prepared to enlarge the funding base for television companies, for there is clearly a limit to the numbers of channels and programs that can be funded by subsidy/license fee alone. By allowing advertising revenue and sponsorship into the television funding mix—be it through public corporations taking advertising or wholly private stations—the potential output and funding base of national TV has risen. However, the expansion of output has rarely, if ever, been matched by a corresponding increase in the capacity of national audiovisual industries to supply all of the potential broadcast slots. Thus, the expansion of television output across and within countries has fueled the demand for television imports. (p. 357)

Adapted from Held, D. et al. (1999). *Global Transformations*. Cambridge: Polity Press.

3.2 Discuss your ideas with another student.

3.3 The concluding sentence in a paragraph can have a number of functions. Complete the following box with some ideas of your own, and then discuss them with your instructor.

Study tip

In Unit 2, we saw how paragraph leaders and topic sentences can help your reader understand the main ideas in a paragraph more clearly. Similarly, a *concluding* sentence can help the reader understand more clearly how you have developed the main idea in a paragraph.

The concluding sentence in a paragraph can:

- summarize the main ideas of your paragraph
- _____
- _____
- _____
- _____
- _____
- _____

3.4 Discuss with your class and instructor whether the concluding sentences in the paragraphs in Ex 3.1 have any of the above functions.

3.5 **The concluding sentences of the following paragraphs from student essays have been removed. Write a suitable concluding sentence for each paragraph.**

1

Global warming has had a number of negative effects on the environment. Agricultural crops have been damaged; for example, last year's rice production decreased, so many people are suffering from famine. Many African countries, especially, have a much lower yield of agricultural production. Furthermore, the sea levels are rising around the world, which has led to the disappearance of many islands. Global warming can also affect people's health, in particular, extremely hot temperatures can increase the number of people who die on any given day. In hot weather the heart needs to work harder, for example. It can also affect the immune system.

_____

_____

_____

2

There are two major reasons for the declining quality in teaching. One problem is the pressure of the increasing population on the demand for school places. This situation has placed excessive strain on the system as it tries to meet these demands, and it has also led to a declining quality in teaching. As a result, although a large proportion of students may enter the school system, only a small percentage proceed to high school level, and an even smaller number finish high school. The other reason is that instructors' salaries are low. Watson (1980) states that "instructors in Thailand remain ill paid"; until more money can be injected into instructors' salaries, thereby attracting better staff, the quality of teaching will remain low, and continue to be one of the causes of poor performance.

_____

_____

_____

3

The development of information technology has meant that many businesses have been able to reduce their running costs. This revolution has helped reduce the need for paper-handling operations and other routine work. Moreover, it has also enabled companies to dismantle their main offices, and thus cut overhead costs, as many employees can now work at home or in satellite offices, using computers and telecommunication devices.

_____

_____

_____

Edited extracts from authentic student material

Task 4: Microskills: Conclusions

4.1 What is the function of a conclusion or concluding paragraph?

_____

_____

_____

_____

4.2 Discuss your ideas with another student.

4.3 Read the following conclusions to an essay with this title: **Is it better to help developing countries to help themselves than to give them food and machinery?** Identify the function(s) of these paragraphs.

1

It seems that in countries with misguided policies, where conventional aid is known to fail, those who want to help should concentrate not on lending money, but on the policy of education. They should advise the governments and help to provide different kinds of training; they should act as vehicles for transferring knowledge. Other types of aid are not useful, as they often support the ineffective economic policies of a government, increase a country's dependence on aid source, and contribute to a waste of money on projects that are not viable. In some cases the consequences of such aid are not prosperity and economic development, but stagnation and an increase in poverty. Before giving financial aid or machinery, the people should be educated in how best to use them, which is the most useful contribution developed countries can make to developing countries.

2

To conclude, it is important to stress that developing countries need help, but it is difficult to decide which is the most effective and appropriate help for any given situation. The countries that want to help are wise to include local people in the early stages of planning an aid project, as this cooperation results in the continuity of the program, and ongoing interest in and maintenance of the project over a long period. So a logical outcome of viewing development aid as a right and not as a gift, is that development cooperation should be based on a genuine partnership, with program ownership and implementation anchored in the developing countries. However, in spite of all these possible solutions, it is the responsibility of developing countries to choose the best way because they know their own situation. They need only to be shown the direction in which to go in order to solve their problems, and then they will be able to achieve their goal.

3

In conclusion, it seems that the roots of the current crisis from which the third world suffers are centuries old, as some of them date from the nineteenth century and are directly linked to colonialism. In spite of all the efforts that have already been made in the economic and social fields, the problems still exist, and if no action is taken within the next few years, the situation will inevitably deteriorate, and even affect the interests of the developed countries, as they will lose the extensive markets that the developing countries represent.

Edited extracts from authentic student material

Key writing skills: The conclusion should signal to your readers that you have finished your writing and should leave them with the clear impression that the purposes of the essay have been achieved. The most common types of conclusions include:

- a summary of the main points (being careful not to repeat exactly what you have written before);
- concluding statements drawn from the points made in the main body;
- recommendations of action to be taken, or suggestions;
- predictions formed from information in the main body;
- solution(s) to a problem or problems described in the main body.

> **Study tip**
>
> An effective conclusion helps your reader to understand the main ideas, and their implications.

It should not include any new important ideas. These ideas should have already been discussed in the main body. Just as an effective introduction progresses from a general statement to a specific thesis statement, so an effective conclusion might progress from a specific statement to a general statement.

4.4 The following sentences form the conclusion to an essay entitled: **The benefits of higher education.** Rearrange the sentences to form a more effective conclusion.

❶ In that sense, educational levels are more likely to be improved and education methods more efficient.

❷ To conclude, it seems that universities and higher education establishments have been of widespread importance in the improvements and developments realized in modern societies.

❸ However, more should be done to ensure further improvement and participation of those bodies in the development process, for instance the cancellation of tuition fees, or at least a reduction.

Edited extracts from authentic student material

4.5 These sentences form the conclusion of an essay entitled: **The consumption of tobacco and its consequences.** Rearrange the sentences to form a more effective conclusion.

❶ However, most people recognize that many developed countries use the international organizations as a curtain to achieve their purposes. This is becaue they are by far the biggest beneficiaries of tobacco production, gaining $100 billion a year from taxes on tobacco.

❷ A rational consideration of this situation should lead to a ban on tobacco consumption being introduced, resulting in fewer deaths from smoking-related illness. However, there are many who believe that, despite repeated efforts to instigate change, the present situation will remain indefinitely.

❸ We have established that there are so many possible solutions to the problems of tobacco consumption that it would be impossible to consider them in an essay of this length.

❹ As discussed in this paper, they often respond to tobacco problems by suggesting solutions that benefit their own interests, rather than those of the developing countries, and they use international organizations to introduce them.

4.6 Look carefully at the conclusion of your essay on statistics and revise it according to the tasks that you have completed in Unit 4.

Unit summary

In this unit you have focused in more depth on how to organize your ideas and include ideas and information from other sources. You have also looked at the functions of concluding sentences and paragraphs.

1   **At the beginning of this unit you read that the unit would help you develop five specific skills. Look back and decide at what stage in the unit you practiced these. Complete the following table with the appropriate activity number.**

Skill	Task / Activity
Deciding what the essay is asking you to write about	
Deciding the most appropriate way of organizing your ideas	
Deciding what information in a text is useful to support your ideas	
Incorporating that information in your writing	
Effectively ending your paragraph with a concluding sentence	
Effectively ending an essay with a conclusion	

2   **Think about the microskills you have learned in this unit. Then complete each bullet point with your own ideas. You may wish to use some of the words in the box.**

complete   appropriate   function   paraphrase   reference   source
quote   accurate   signal   specific   general   new ideas

- Each paragraph in an academic essay should have a concluding sentence that

  _____

- If you incorporate information from texts into your essay, you need to

  _____.

- The conclusion to your essay should _____

  It should *not* _____

For web resources relevant to this unit, see:

www.englishforacademicstudy.com/us/student/writing/links

5 Human Activity and Climate Change

This unit will help you:
- practice writing clear definitions;
- learn how to support and develop your ideas.

Text 5 | Human activity and climate change (pp. 184–191)

During this task, you will have an opportunity to read extracts from a brochure co-sponsored by the United Nations Environmental Programme (UNEP) and the World Meteorological Organization (WMO).

Task 1: Microskills: Short definitions

Read Texts 5-1 to 5-4, entitled *Human activity and climate change*, and identify information that is relevant to the title of this essay:

> What role has human activity played in causing climate change?

You will now practice some useful skills that you can incorporate in the first draft of your essay.

1.1 **Think about the following definition of an instructor.**

An instructor is a person who teaches.

a) Is it a suitable definition or not?

b) If it is, why? If it isn't, why not?

c) Discuss your ideas with another student.

1.2 **With your partner, discuss when you need to define a word, or terminology, in academic life. Think about this in a variety of contexts, spoken as well as written.**

1.3 **Look at the following list of words and the context in which they are being used. Which of the words do you think you need to define and why?**

a)	**gene**	You are a genetic engineer writing an article for a biotechnology journal.
b)	**nurture**	You are an ESL student writing for a non-specialist readership.
c)	**migration**	You are a sociologist writing a first-year undergraduate textbook.
d)	**education**	You are an ESL student writing an essay on *Which form or forms of education contribute to the social and economic development of a society?*
e)	**globalization**	You are a university professor writing an article on the impact of economic globalization on developing countries for an international relations journal.

f) **particle physics**   You are a journalist writing an article for a quality newspaper.

g) **desertification**   You are a professor of geography writing a college textbook about the changing climate in Central Africa.

h) **skimming**   You are an English-language instructor writing a book on *How to read efficiently*.

1.4 **Discuss your ideas with your partner. Try to reach an agreement about the reasons for your choice.**

1.5 **Choose four of the words in Ex 1.3 and write a definition of them.**

_____

_____

_____

_____

_____

Key writing skills: The amount and nature of the information that a writer gives in a definition will depend on:

● whether the concept is considered to be new for the readers;

● how much knowledge of the concept it is thought the readers will already have.

1.6 **How could you improve the following definitions and make them more "honest," or less dogmatic?**

a) Globalization is the intensification of economic, political, social, and cultural relations across borders.

b) The developing countries are those countries that were previously colonized.

c) Subsistence farming is when rural communities have grown their own food.

Formal definitions

The definitions given in Ex 1.6 are known as *formal* definitions. This means that they follow a particular pattern of sentence structure.

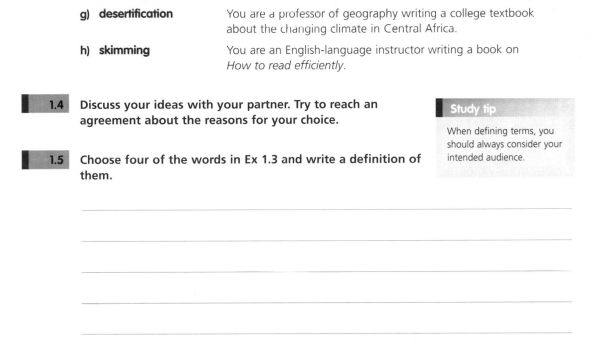

1		2		3
name of the term being defined	**+ verb**	**class to which it belongs**	**+ *who/which that/where***	**special features**

If you use an expression like *may be defined as* or *can be defined as* instead of the verb *to be*, you are being more honest and accepting that there can be alternative definitions.

Example:

A triangle may be *defined* as a geometric figure that has three straight sides, and three angles.

1.7 Write a formal definition for the following words:

a) square

b) television

c) dictionary

_____

_____

_____

_____

_____

_____

Naming definitions

The three elements that make up a formal definition can be put in a different order to give *a naming definition*.

2		3		1
class to which it belongs	*+ who/which that/where*	**special features**	*+ verb*	**name of the term being defined**

In a naming definition, the verb is passive, e.g., *may be called* or *may be named*.

Example:

A geometric figure that has three straight sides and three angles *may be called* a triangle.

1.8 In Ex 1.7 you wrote three formal definitions. Now write three naming definitions for the same words.

_____

_____

_____

Study tip
In formal definitions, the special features are emphasized, while in a naming definition it is the name of the thing being defined that is emphasized.

_____

_____

_____

_____

1.9   Study the four definitions below. Are they formal or naming definitions? Write F (formal) or N (naming).

1

The period after independence is sometimes called neo-colonialism—the continuation of colonial exploitation without formal political control. This concept also covers the relationship of the third world with the United States, which (with a few exceptions) was not a formal colonizer in the first place. And it covers the North–South international relations of Latin American states that have been independent for almost two centuries. _____

2

Biodiversity is the tremendous diversity of plant and animal species making up the Earth's (global, regional and local) ecosystems. _____

3

The massive transfer of agricultural technology coordinated through international agencies is called the green revolution. _____

4

Refugees are people fleeing to find refuge from war, natural disaster or political persecution. _____

Goldstein, J.S. (1996). *International Relations* (pp. 484, 434, 531, 496). New York: Harper Collins.

1.10   Find two definitions in Text 5. Are they formal or naming definitions?

Task 2: Extended definitions

2.1   Think of two different ways in which a definition could be extended. Discuss your ideas with the class.

2.2   Look at the following two extracts. How have the definitions been extended?

1

Technological transfer refers to a third-world state's acquisition of technology (knowledge, skills, methods, designs, specialized equipment, and so on) from foreign sources, usually in conjunction with direct foreign investment or similar business operations. For example, a third world state may allow an MNC to produce certain goods in the country under favorable conditions, provided the MNC shares knowledge of the technology and design behind the product. The state may try to get its own citizens into the management and professional workforce of factories or facilities created by foreign investment. In this way not only does physical capital accumulate in the country, so does the related technological base for further development. However, MNCs are sometimes reluctant to share proprietary technology.

(Goldstein, 1996, p. 531)   (MNC = multinational corporation)

2

In the field of International Relations governmental loans are funds given to help in economic development, which must be repaid in the future out of the surplus generated by the development process ... unlike commercial loans, government-to-government development loans are often on subsidized terms, with long repayment times and low interest rates. Although still an obligation for the recipient country, such loans are relatively easy to service and thus do not hold back the country's accumulation of surplus in the short term.

(Goldstein, 1996, p. 541)

Reading & Writing

2.3 Read the following definitions.

❶
Anthropology may be defined as a branch of both science and sociology in which people, society, and culture are studied.

❷
Physics may be defined as a branch of science in which forces such as heat, light, sound, pressure, gravity and electricity, and the way that they affect objects are studied.

a) What is being defined in each definition?

b) Why do you think the subjects are defined as a branch of a wider subject?

Note that if you are in an academic environment with other students who are going to study a different subject from yours, you may want to explain your subject to them.

2.4 Study the following definition of psychology. How has it been extended and how do you expect the writer to continue?

Psychology may be defined as the science that studies the behavior of man and other animals. For this definition to be useful, it is necessary to specify more clearly what psychologists mean by behavior. An idea of the meaning of behavior can be gained if the topics covered by psychology are examined: the behaving organism, growth and development, motivation and emotion, perception learning and thinking, individuality and personality, conflict, adjustment and mental health, and social aspects of psychology. The behaving organism is important because, as a science rooted in biology, psychology is interested in the bodily processes that make activity possible ...

Buzan, T. (1971). *Speed Reading*. USA: David and Charles.

2.5 Now write an extended definition of your subject. Compare with another student and discuss any difficulties you had.

_____

_____

_____

2.6 What definitions do you think would be useful to use in your essay on climate change? Write those definitions.

_____

_____

_____

_____

_____

Task 3: Microskills: Exemplification and support

You are probably aware of how important it is to support the idea(s) expressed in your topic sentence with examples and details. In this task you will look at ways of doing this by analyzing paragraphs from student essays.

3.1 **Read the following paragraphs from student essays entitled Is it beneficial or detrimental to a country to have more than one ethnic group? Then decide whether you are satisfied that you have completely understood the writer's idea(s).**

a) If so, why?

b) If not, why not?

❶

> Since the Meiji Revolution, a revolution of democracy, every Japanese citizen is supposed to be considered equal, as there is no longer a class system in Japan. The people called "burakumin" are the descendents of the former cattle slaughterers, tanners, and grave diggers, jobs that were considered impure and dirty. Unemployment is not the only problem they face: for example, intermarriage with other ethnic groups is seen to be undesirable.

❷

> A country's power structure seems to be linked with its multi-ethnic struggle because nowadays a multi-ethnic structure in a country seems to create racism. For instance, in Turkey, the ethnic group of the Kurds continues its conflict over their sovereignty with the Turkish, Iranian, and Iraqi governments. Each ethnic group has its own culture, such as language, traditional lifestyle, and social discipline; however, a country's policy naturally tends towards offering maximum benefit to the majority groups. Thus, a minority group like the Kurds feel that their rights have been infringed. Considering this aspect, a multi-ethnic structure in a country could be considered to be detrimental to a cohesive society.

Edited extracts from authentic student material

3.2 **Discuss your ideas with another student.**

3.3 **There are different ways of supporting a main point. Think about how the writers illustrated/supported their main points in the following paragraphs.**

❶

> In the last twenty years, a series of technological and political changes have transformed the televisual landscape and have contributed to the globalization of television as a medium and as an industry. First and foremost, the number of countries with broadcasting systems and the number of televisions available on which to watch their output has steadily risen. From its Western core, television has spread in the postwar years across Eastern Europe and the Soviet Union, into Latin America, Asia, and Africa. Second, within the West, but later in other areas as well, the number of terrestrial channels has steadily climbed. In part, this has been because governments have been prepared to enlarge the funding base for television companies, for there is clearly a limit to the number of channels and programs that can be funded by subsidy/license fee alone. By allowing advertising revenue and sponsorship into the television funding mix—be it through public corporations taking advertising or wholly private stations—the potential output and funding base of national television has risen. However, the expansion of output has rarely, if ever, been matched by a corresponding increase in the capacity of national audiovisual industries to supply all of the potential broadcast slots. Thus the expansion of television output across and within countries has fueled the demand for television imports.

Held, D. et al. (1999). *Global Transformations*. Cambridge: Polity Press.

❷ Indonesia has a population of approximately 200 million, among which there are many ethnic groups. According to the research of Smith and Wallis (1996), Indonesia has 365 ethnic groups, of which four are major groups. They are Javanese (about 45%), Sundanese (about 14%), Madurese (7.5%) and Malay (7.5%). The other ethnic groups make up about 26%. The main group, the Javanese, do not only live on Java Island, but are spread among other islands. This situation has been caused by the government's 1977 emigration program by which many Javanese left Java to live on other islands, such as Sumatra, Kalimantan and Irian Jaya. They found jobs mainly in government positions or as business entrepreneurs in all the main cities of Indonesia. Thus, as the majority group in each city, the Javanese became very influential.

Edited extracts from authentic student material

3.4 Bearing in mind the extracts in Ex 3.3, discuss with your partner the different ways you can support and develop your ideas.

3.5 Read the following sentences from Ex 3.1 ❷ and Ex 3.3 ❷. Do they contain a statement of fact or opinion?

A country's power structure seems to be linked with its multiethnic struggle, because nowadays a multiethnic structure in a country seems to create racism.

Indonesia has a population of approximately 200 million, among which there are many ethnic groups.

Study tip

It is important to use examples, figures, or statistics to add support to and develop your ideas, whether they are fact or opinion. This will help the reader understand your line of argument.

Supporting with examples

3.6 Note down some expressions that can introduce an example into your writing.

_____

_____

_____

_____

3.7 Compare your expressions with the ones your instructor will give you.

3.8 Complete each of the following texts using one of the expressions. Do not use an expression more than once. Note that there is one expression that you will not use.

❶ Nowadays, tobacco is grown in more than a hundred countries, and it is the chief product and commodity of exportation for many countries, especially those in the global south; _____ is in Africa, where the crop is grown on millions of hectares and the industry employs a large amount of the local manpower.

❷ In addition to the limitations on advertising and promotional campaigns, some governments require tobacco companies with significant sales to develop national multimedia campaigns to educate young people about the real health dangers associated with tobacco use. _____ in the US, a company had spent $150 million on such a campaign by 1999.

❸ Even though there are many reports that, on average, regular smokers are more likely to develop lung and heart disease, tobacco is still being produced in, and exported from, many countries. _____ in 1990, China produced 40% of the total world output of about six million tons, the US produced 223 thousand tons, Brazil produced 188 thousand tons, and Italy produced 138 thousand tons.

❹ However, sometimes the fax machine and e-mail are used in a negative way, _____ the delivery of junk and abusive mail, as it is difficult to discover the sender.

❺ One advantage of having an open market is the fact that new companies can enter the market, so the customer can have a wider choice of product. There will also be more competition between the companies to create the best product, thus eliminating low-quality products from the market. _____ is the growing market for mobile phones in Colombia. Two companies are trying to enter the market by offering free mobile phones.

Supporting with chronological markers

3.9 Read the following first sentence of a paragraph. It is the paragraph leader. Continue the paragraph, supporting the idea in the paragraph leader in an appropriate way.

> The communications revolution has affected the lives of ordinary citizens in a
> number of ways.

3.10 Use the following statistics on travel expenditure in the UK to write a paragraph that develops the following topic sentence:

> The weekly expenditure on travel and leisure of single males and females is very different.

Weekly expenditure on travel and leisure in the United Kingdom by gender, 1999–2000		
	Men* $ per week	Women* $ per week
Motoring, fares and other travel costs	78.60	60.30
Alcohol and tobacco	36.70	18.00
TV, video, computers and audio**	17.20	9.20
Clothing and footwear	15.00	23.40
Vacations	9.40	10.40
Books and magazines	4.90	4.60
Sports admissions and subscriptions	4.70	2.00
Gambling	4.40	2.30
Toiletries and beauty products	3.00	9.50
Other leisure	7.00	9.20
All expenditure on travel and leisure	**180.90**	**148.90**

*   households headed by a single non-retired person, aged 16 and over with no children
** includes rental

**Source: Adapted from *Family Expenditure Survey*, Office for National Statistics
(http://www.statistics.gov.uk/statbase/xsdataset.asp)**

Task 4: Writing your essay

4.1 Look at the plan for your essay for Unit 5. How could you improve the quality of your essay by incorporating definitions and support for your ideas?

4.2 Now write the first draft of your essay.

4.3 When you have finished your first draft, find another student who has finished and exchange drafts.

a) Read your partner's draft carefully.

b) Respond to the questions on the Peer Evaluation Sheet for Unit 5 on page 144.

Unit summary

In this unit you have practiced writing definitions. You have also focused on how to develop your ideas by using background support and examples.

1   **How could you explain the following to another student?**

a)   a formal definition

_____

b)   a naming definition

_____

c)   an honest definition

_____

d)   an extended definition

_____

2   **Identify the function of the underlined sections in each extract below.**

a)   … In the last ten years, the landscape has been transformed. <u>First</u>, the number of households using the technology has increased … .

b)   … Recently there has been substantial population growth. <u>There have been several surveys that indicate</u> … .

c)   … The open market has certain disadvantages. <u>A case in point is</u> …

d)   … Expenditure on leisure increases during the summer. <u>This is due to</u> increased tourism … .

3   **Complete this summary using your own words:**

This unit has helped me become more aware of how to develop my ideas in an essay more effectively by:

_____

_____

_____

For web resources relevant to this unit, see:
www.englishforacademicstudy.com/us/student/writing/links

The Global Village

This unit will help you:
- learn how to choose appropriate patterns of organizing the content of your essays;
- practice incorporating ideas from your reading into your writing.

Task 1: Microskills: Organizing essays of cause and effect

One common approach to problem solving in academic life is to examine the causes and effects of situations. When expressing these in writing, you need to use appropriate patterns of content organization, and appropriate language; this makes the link between the cause and effect clear and explicit. You will explore this approach in Unit 6.

1.1 **Read the following student essay entitled: Discuss the positive and negative effects of tourism on people and the environment. Identify the purpose of each paragraph.**
Write notes in the margin and underline key points that help you decide.

❶
Since the end of World War II, the developed countries have made very significant leaps in progress. <u>A consequence of</u> this development for the populations of these countries has been that their standards of living have risen year after year. They have now reached a situation in which most of the people are living a healthy and comfortable life. Parallel to the rise in standards of living, many people have developed a strong desire to visit different parts of the world, resulting in a steep rise in foreign tourism. Nowadays, it is common for people to take a vacation in a foreign country rather than in their own native country. This essay will attempt to discuss the effects of tourism on people and the environment.

❷
Most people tend to take a vacation at least once a year; for some people it is almost a duty. <u>Owing to</u> the rising standards of living, people, especially from the developed countries, do not hesitate to spend large amounts of money on the pleasure of having a break far from their permanent residence. Travel agencies and tourism companies have capitalized on this trend; they display advertisements with attractive pictures, and offer affordable prices with the aim of enticing more people to travel the world on their vacation. <u>This has caused</u> the number of people who travel for their vacations to multiply many times over the last few decades. As vacationers tend to travel to tropical areas and coastal towns where they can enjoy permanent sunshine, beaches, or extensive forest areas, it seems that no part of the world has been untouched by tourism.

3

The millions of vacationers who travel the world looking for new places have caused serious problems for the local population and for the environment of the destination countries. In fact, one result of the rising numbers of tourists visiting developing countries is that a certain proportion of the local population has developed illegal activities. For instance, the trade in ivory products has increased at the expense of elephants, especially in the Ivory Coast and Kenya. Another example is the trade in Siberian tiger furs, which is threatening the species with extinction. Worse still, particularly in South Asia, the population has suffered from the rapid proliferation of prostitution, mainly due to the large number of people operating sex tourism. Thailand, where minors are occasionally sold by their parents, is a case in point.

4

Another harmful effect of tourism is the damage it causes to the environment. In fact, as a result of the large number of tourists visiting some parts of the world, environmental damage has reached serious proportions and natural resources have been degraded. An example of this is the Mediterranean Sea, which is reported to be the dirtiest sea in the world because of sewage contamination; German coasts have also been polluted by effluent from the many cruising boats; in France, where sewage is sometimes discharged directly into streams, most of those in the Pyrenees are now polluted. Above all, the dense aerial traffic created by the active movement of vacationers has caused an alarming rise in air pollution; this gives rise to acid rain that, in turn, contaminates soils and causes serious damage to forest areas. For example, 60% of the Alpine forests in France are reported to be experiencing serious degradation. So it would seem that mass tourism has resulted in very serious problems for both the people and the environment of the destination countries.

5

The rising intensity of the threat that mass tourism represents has prompted some governments and non-governmental organizations to act swiftly. In fact, some governments have made considerable efforts to sensitize their population to the threat that tourism represents to the environment; campaigns have been launched and money has been spent to protect the environment and to counteract the environmental damage that has already occurred. In France, for example, the government spends billions of euros on ways to protect the national nature reserves and tidy the beaches and mountain villages from tourist-related waste. It is also engaged in creating tree plantations to replace trees destroyed by acid rain. In York, in England, many residents wear anti-tourist badges in protest against the increase in the number of tourists. Access to many monuments, such as the Leaning Tower of Pisa in Italy and the Parthenon in Athens, is extremely restricted. In addition, local governments in Africa, with the help of non-governmental organizations like Greenpeace, have declared war on the illegal trade in ivory and the fur from wild animals that are currently menaced with extinction. It therefore seems that significant effort has been made in different parts of the world where nature appears to be threatened.

6

The solutions that have been adopted by governments have not shown much effectiveness or efficiency, however. Although governments have made serious efforts to deal with the problems, sometimes by enacting strict new laws, mass tourism is still causing many problems, and the intensity of degradation that has been registered in the environment has not declined. Also, the traffic in ivory and rare animal furs has considerably increased, and gangs are becoming more organized because of the potential profits that can be obtained from this traffic. The strict laws do not seem to dissuade the gangs from carrying out these illegal and destructive activities. In addition, in spite of the huge efforts made by the international courts and the organizations for the protection and promotion of children's rights, there are still hundreds of thousands of tourists who are reported to practice sex tourism and to abuse poverty. In addition, there is a marked deterioration in the behavior of young people associated with tourism, such as alcohol-related problems and violence, which governments have been unable to prevent despite their efforts to do so.

_____

_____

7

This essay has provided an illustration of the problems generated by mass tourism nowadays, outlined the laws and initiatives adopted by governments and international non-governmental organizations to abolish these problems, and evaluated the solutions. At present, a variety of wild animals and flora is seriously threatened with extinction, the deterioration of sea water has already caused the extinction of some sea species, and the world is losing a forest the size of Britain every year. If nothing is done in the next few years, the worst possible outcome is to be expected, and more destruction is likely to occur to nature and humanity. The underlying causes of these problems require more serious attention, and greater consideration should be paid to the initiatives introduced to solve the problems.

_____

_____

Edited extracts from authentic student material

1.2   **Look back at the title in Ex 1.1 and decide whether the writer has addressed all the parts of the question. For example:**

- Are all the paragraphs necessary?
- Are all the relevant points appropriately developed?

What other questions can you ask to evaluate the success of this essay?

1.3 There are a number of different ways of developing an essay involving an explanation and analysis of the causes and effects of a situation. Study the two simplest models set out below. Then think about them in relation to the essay you have just read.

a) Which of the two models is most similar to the essay?

b) What are the advantages and disadvantages of each pattern?

1

Paragraph 1	Introduction (which introduces the situation to the reader)
Paragraph 2	Causes
Paragraph 3	Causes
Paragraph 4	Causes
Paragraph 5	Transition paragraph
Paragraph 6	Effects
Paragraph 7	Effects
Paragraph 8	Effects
Paragraph 9	Evaluation
Paragraph 10	Conclusion

2

Paragraph 1	Introduction
Paragraph 2	Cause/Effect
Paragraph 3	Cause/Effect
Paragraph 4	Cause/Effect
Paragraph 5	Evaluation
Paragraph 6	Conclusion

1.4 Discuss your answers with another student.

1.5 Look at the underlined words in Ex 1.1. What purpose do these expressions have within or between the sentences?

a) Find similar expressions with the same function in paragraphs 3, 4 and 5.

b) Note down more such expressions.

c) Compare your answers with your partner.

Write ten sentences to connect the following ideas using some of the expressions discussed in Ex 1.5.

Examples: **air travel—airports.** Since there is such a demand for air travel, the government is building more airports.

Infected mosquitos—malaria. Due to the rising number of infected mosquitoes, malaria has become an even worse threat to health than in the 1990s.

a) rain—floods _____

_____

b) globalization—cultural convergence _____

_____

c) fear—adrenalin _____

_____

d) inflation—unemployment _____

_____

e) arid climate—irrigate fields _____

_____

f) absenteeism—low productivity _____

_____

g) lack of plants—soil erosion _____

_____

h) satellites—mobile phones _____

_____

i) high birth rate—overcrowding _____

_____

Language to express cause and effect

Here are some useful expressions commonly used when expressing cause and effect:

A   Using *cause* as a noun

	direct	
The	likely	cause of death was a serious bacterial infection.
	major	
	main	

The cause of the damage was not known.

Structure: The + (adjective) + cause + of + noun + verb to be + noun clause

B   Using *reason* as a noun

	main	
The	first/second/third	reason for choosing a university is its academic reputation.

| One | key | reason for entering higher education is to improve |

employment prospects.

Structure: The + (adjective) + reason + for + _____ ing + noun +
verb to be + noun phrase/verb phrase

Many young couples are not able to buy their own home.
The reason for this situation is the rising price of housing.

Structure: The + (adjective) + reason + for + noun + verb to be + noun phrase/verb phrase

C   Using *cause* as a verb

	may	
Loans	can	cause financial problems for some students.
	will	

Falls in the Asian stock market may cause significant damage to markets in
the United States and Europe.

Structure: noun + (modal auxiliary verb) + cause + noun phrase

D   Using *result* as a verb

The rise in house prices may/can/will result in fewer young people buying their first home.

Structure: Noun phrase + (modal) result + in + noun phrase

E   Using *effect* (noun) pattern 1

The effect of loan sales is an immediate improvement in the public finances.

The effect of greenhouse gases is to warm the atmosphere.

Structure: The + (adjective) + effect of noun + verb to be + noun phrase/verb phrase

F   Using *effect* (noun) pattern 2

Violence on television can have a(n)	substantial	effect on the behavior of children.
	adverse	
	strong	

Loans may have a disincentive effect on the willingness of individuals from low socioeconomic groups to participate in higher education.

Structure: noun + (modal auxiliary verb) + have + a/an + (adjective) + effect + on + noun phrase

G   Using *affect* (verb)

The increase in greenhouse gases in the atmosphere significantly affects some of the continental scale patterns of climate change.

Adverse weather conditions can affect the psychological state of human beings.

Structure: noun +	adverb	+ affect(s) + noun phrase
	modal auxiliary	

H   Using the first conditional

When there is a dense accumulation of pollutants in the air, people often become ill.

When a reduction in the research funds available occurs, there is a decrease in the number of medical research projects.

Structure: When + cause + effect

Text 6 | The global village (pp. 192–205)

The text deals with the effects of globalization on the world we live in and contains information relevant to your essay.

Task 2: Writing your essay

2.1 **You are going to write an essay on the following topic:**

> *Discuss the positive and negative effects of globalization on the world today.*

Quickly decide with another student what the question is asking you to do.

2.2 **Read Text 6 entitled The global village. Then brainstorm ideas in order to develop further ideas for your essay, considering the information you read in the text.**

2.3 **Decide which pattern of organization is most appropriate for your essay. Organize your ideas in a plan.**

2.4 **Exchange plans with another student and evaluate each other's plans.**

2.5 **Write your first draft.**

2.6 **When you have finished your first draft, find another student who has finished and exchange drafts.**

a) Read your partner's draft carefully.

b) Respond to the questions on the Peer Evaluation Sheet for Unit 6 on page 145.

2.7 **Write your second draft.**

Unit summary

In this unit you have looked at different ways of organizing the contents of an essay. You have also worked on incorporating ideas from your reading into your essay.

1 **Think about and/or discuss your answers to the following questions.**

a) I have trouble knowing when to start a new paragraph when I write essays. Will it help if I use the same basic paragraph organization for all my essays?

b) My essay is supposed to be on the advantages and disadvantages of tourism in developing countries, but I can't think of many disadvantages. How important is it to look at negative effects as well as positive ones?

c) How flexible should the plan for my essay be? For example, do I have to have three paragraphs on the advantages of a situation, and three paragraphs on the disadvantages?

d) Why is it important to use particular language patterns in different types of essays? For example, in a cause and effect essay, do I need to use the language expressions on pages 130–132? Should I vary the expressions I use—I get confused about the different grammar patterns.

2 **Choose the best option to complete the sentences below.**

a) The decision on how to organize your essay should depend on *the topic of the essay / your instructor's preference*.

b) You need to plan your paragraphs and edit them after you have written your first draft so that each paragraph has a clear *ending / function*.

c) It is important to answer the essay question fully and give a balanced answer. For example, if you are asked to discuss advantages and disadvantages, *you should try to / don't need to* give equal attention to both sides of the argument.

d) You can use different patterns to organize your essays. As you become more skilled and confident you can *be more flexible / write longer paragraphs*.

e) If you are aware of and able to use common essay-writing expressions, it will make the ideas in your essay *less exciting and original / clearer and easier to follow*.

For web resources relevant to this unit, see:
www.englishforacademicstudy.com/us/student/writing/links

7 The New Linguistic Order

In this unit you will:
- choose an essay to write based on the topic of either globalization or the rise of English as a world language;
- learn how to choose appropriate patterns of organizing the content of your essays;
- further practice incorporating ideas from your reading into your writing.

Task 1: Microskills: Organizing essays: Situation, problems, solutions, implications, evaluation

Another common approach to problem solving in academic life is to examine the problems that have arisen from a specific situation, suggest solutions to the problems, look at the implications of the suggested solutions, and evaluate these. When expressing this approach in writing, you need to make choices as to the most appropriate way of organizing the information in your writing and the most appropriate language to use to express your ideas. You will explore some of these ways in this unit.

1.1 **Look at the pattern in the box below. This shows how the above is reflected in the organization of text. Think about how this organization has been applied in the sample text.**

> Situation ➡ Problems ➡ Solutions ➡ Implications ➡ Evaluation

> I am a foreign student living in the United States. I find it very difficult to meet American students and so cannot make American friends and practice my English. I will join some university clubs so as to meet some students. This should help to put me in contact with American students. I should then be able to make friends and improve my English.

Key writing skill: The above approach is a very common way of organizing ideas in academic writing and can be used for:

- a paragraph;
- a section of a longer document;
- a complete article;
- a complete book.

1.2 **Think of a situation that you have been in that has led to a problem (different from the example above). Write a short paragraph that introduces the situation, explains the problem, suggests a solution, states the implications, and evaluates the outcome.**

1.3 Read the following article about global migration. Identify how the pattern described in Ex 1.1 and 1.2 is used in the article.

GLOBAL MIGRATION

The movement of populations across borders has increased to such an extent as to produce a global migration crisis. As a result of this development, a number of ethical issues have arisen, such as the proportion of ethnic groups within a country, the national identity of a country, racism, the effect of a multicultural society, and the distribution of wealth. It is mainly the governments of the host countries that seek to solve these problems by establishing language programs, cultural exchange and awareness-raising programs and, where possible, employment opportunities. However, if this pattern of migration continues, there needs to be more openness and willingness on behalf of the native population to accept and receive migrants into their society, and to realize the benefits that a multicultural society can bring. The implications of this suggestion are wide, and not without problems: many older people are resistant to change, and the working population are resistant to outside competition for employment opportunities. There also needs to be a much higher level of cooperation between the host country and the country of origin in order to establish a clear identity for the migrants.

It is obvious that any solution to the problems mentioned above will involve much greater cooperation at the levels of citizens, ethnic groups, and political bodies; it will also take many years for any adjustment to take place. However, it is hoped that over time, and with greater understanding of the global picture and the possibility of a global governing body that is fair to all global citizens, the problems resulting from the issues of global migration will be minimized.

1.4 Complete the flow diagram using information from the text above.

> **Situation:** _____
>
> ⬇
>
> **Problem(s):** _____
>
> ⬇
>
> **Solution(s):** _____
>
> ⬇
>
> **Implication(s):** _____
>
> ⬇
>
> **Evaluation:** _____

1.5 Compare your answers with another student.

1.6 Is there a further problem created by the proposed solution in the text?

1.7 What language do you think it is appropriate to use when giving an evaluation?

Text 7 | The new linguistic order (pp. 206–214)

This text comes from an article in the magazine *Foreign Policy* and contains information relevant to your essay.

Task 2: Writing your essay

2.1 Read Text 7. Then reread Text 6 entitled *The global village*. These will help you respond to the following tasks.
You should use the information from both texts, and any of your own texts, to support the ideas in your essay.

2.2 Choose one of the following essays, then brainstorm your ideas.

❶ The process of globalization has given rise to a number of problems. Identify one of these problems, explain the situation that gave rise to the problem and offer some solutions. You should also evaluate your solutions.

❷ It could be said that globalization has increased the gap between the "haves" and the "have nots," and that this is a problem. Explain how this situation has arisen and offer some solutions to this problem. You should also evaluate your solutions.

❸ There are a number of problems associated with the rise of English as a world language. Outline some of these problems, explain how they arose, offer some solutions and evaluate your proposed solutions.

2.3 Plan your essay, thinking about the order and grouping of your ideas.

● Try to arrange your ideas in a logical order.

● Decide how your points can be grouped together, so that each group has one main or unifying idea.

● Decide how your groups of points can be arranged effectively in a
Situation ➡ Problems ➡ Solutions ➡ Implications ➡ Evaluation pattern.

2.4 Exchange plans with another student and evaluate her/his plan.

2.5 Write the first draft of your essay. Aim to write at least 1,000 words.

2.6 When you have finished your first draft, find another student who has finished and exchange drafts.

a) Evaluate her/his draft.

b) Write your second draft, aiming to improve the development of your ideas.

Unit summary

In this unit you have looked at more ways of organizing essays appropriately. You have also practiced writing an essay using the pattern: situation-problem-solution-implications-evaluation.

1 **Think about the essay you wrote in Task 2 and reflect on or discuss the questions.**

a) How did Task 1 help you plan your essay?

b) How easy did you find it to plan and organize your essays?

c) How effectively did you incorporate ideas from the texts you read into your essay?

d) How was the peer evaluation stage of the process useful?

e) Were there any language problems in your essay? How could you avoid this in future?

For web resources relevant to this unit, see:
www.englishforacademicstudy.com/us/student/writing/links

Course summary

The table in Appendix 3 is to help you reflect on your progress during the course. Completing the table will help you assess your strengths and weaknesses, so that you can continue to improve your academic writing.

g Glossary

Anecdote
A short account of an incident that is amusing or interesting.

Academic evidence
Evidence that comes from recognized academic research or published text and is considered to be stronger and more reliable than other forms of evidence.

Analogy
To make or draw an analogy between two things is to show they are alike in some way.

Assumption
If you make an assumption that something is true, you accept it is true without any real proof or evidence.

Brainstorm
To reflect on a topic or issue and generate a large number of ideas. This can be an individual activity or a group activity in which everyone suggests as many possible ways to solve a problem or complete a task as they can.

Chronological marker
A series of words or phrases in a text that indicate how events or ideas are sequenced, e.g., First, second, next, etc.

Citation
A reference to the source of an idea in someone's work. This may be an in-text reference to an author, a reference in a bibliography or footnote or a verbal reference in a talk or lecture.

Complex sentence
A sentence that is made up of two or more clauses, at least one of which must be a dependent clause. It may also include long phrases or unusual syntax and/or terminology. Example: Crime statistics are proof positive that, with a bit of art, you can fool all the people all the time.

Concise (style)
Expressing a lot of information in a few words.

Constructive criticism
Advice that is useful and intended to help someone or improve something. Constructive criticism may also involve offering possible solutions to problems.

Critical reading
Reading in a way that involves questioning what the text says, what the writer is trying to do, and how s/he does this.

Critical stance
To take a critical stance is to have a strong viewpoint on something after examining and judging it carefully.

Critical thinking
Thinking critically involves the following skills: supporting your own views with a clear rationale, evaluating ideas that you hear and read, and making connections between ideas.

Discourse community
People who share similar thoughts and ideas. A discourse community uses particular language, stylistic features, or conventions when its members communicate with each other.

Exploring issues
Looking at issues in some depth and finding out more about them.

Extended definition

This is longer and more detailed than a simple dictionary-style definition. There may be extended examples and/or a contrast with other similar, but distinct concepts in an extended definition.

Genre

A type of text or art form that uses a particular style of writing or speaking. Scientific essays are a different genre from humanities essays.

Manipulate

To adapt or change something (figures, statistics, facts, etc.) so that it shows what you want it to.

Micro-skills

Skills that contribute to a larger or macro skill such as reading, writing, listening, or speaking. Writing micro-skills include organizing and linking ideas.

Paragraph leader

The first sentence in a written paragraph. The paragraph leader links to the ideas in the previous paragraph and may lead into the ideas to be developed in the next paragraph. It is a cohesive device.

Peer evaluation

Peer evaluation takes place when a colleague or another student reads and evaluates the effectiveness of one's work. Peers are often able to suggest improvements quickly.

Process approach

An approach based on the idea that good writers go through a number of processes while composing a text before they produce their final product. It encourages the student to go back to look at and change the text as much as they need to.

Recursive process

A recursive process is one that involves going back and repeating steps. Writing is recursive because it can be improved by frequent editing and revising.

Terminology

Vocabulary (or terms) used in a particular field, topic, or area of study. These may be technical words or terms to describe complex concepts that are specific to that topic.

Thesis

A writer's point of view or position in a text is what may be referred to as her/his thesis. In order to write an evaluative project, the writer needs to develop a thesis as the starting point.

Thesis statement

A statement of the writer's <u>thesis</u>. It is often stated in the introduction and supported by reasons in the body of the essay or presentation, and it is revisited in the conclusion.

Topic sentence

A sentence in a paragraph that directs the ideas that are developed in the paragraph. It is important because it explains the main idea in the paragraph and helps the reader to focus on it.

Trend

A pattern or movement in a particular direction.

PEER EVALUATION SHEET: Unit 1

ESSAY: *What are the aims of academic study and how can they be achieved?*

Task 1

Read your partner's draft carefully. Then read the following questions and reread the parts of the essay that will enable you to answer the questions below.

1.1   Introduction:

a)   Does the essay have an introduction?

b)   Does the introduction explain clearly to the reader what the topic of the essay is? If so, how has the writer achieved this?

c)   What could the writer do to improve it?

1.2   Paragraphing:

a)   Are the ideas in the essay grouped effectively into paragraphs?

b)   If not, does the writer need to change the order of ideas?

c)   Does the writer explain enough about the main idea in each paragraph to make it clear to the reader?

1.3   Conclusion:

Do you feel, as the reader, that there is a suitable conclusion to the essay that refers back to the main ideas of the essay?

1.4   Additional information:

What additional information from the text you have read on academic success could be incorporated into the second draft of the essay?

Task 2

Now discuss each other's drafts. Try to comment on both the strengths and weaknesses in your partner's draft. Ask each other questions like:

●   Why did you begin as you did?

●   Why did you organize the ideas in the way you did?

●   What is the most important idea in your draft?

●   What do you mean by this point?

If points are not clear, or if the writer's main ideas are not clear, discuss these and suggest ways of making them clearer.

Task 3

Consider your partner's comments carefully. Which comments do you agree with? Why? Which comments do you disagree with? Why?

Rewrite your draft, incorporating all the improvements you have discussed and considered.

PEER EVALUATION SHEET: Unit 2

ESSAY: Nurture strongly influences early human development. Discuss.

Task 1

Read your partner's draft carefully. Then read the following questions and reread the parts of the essay that will enable you to answer them:

1.1 Introduction:

a) Does the introduction start with a general statement related to the topic and gradually become more specific?

b) Is there a thesis statement that tells the reader what the essay will be about?

c) Does the essay explain what the thesis statement said it would?

d) What could the writer do to improve it?

1.2 Paragraphing:

a) Are the ideas in the essay grouped effectively into paragraphs?

b) If not, does the writer need to change the order of ideas?

c) Does each paragraph have a paragraph leader that tells the reader what the main idea of the paragraph is?

d) What is the function of each paragraph leader?

e) Does the writer explain enough about the main idea in each paragraph to make it clear to the reader?

f) If not, does the writer need to add further information or examples to make a point clearer?

g) Does the writer need to remove unnecessary information?

1.3 Argument:

a) Is the writer's argument clear throughout the essay?

b) Is the writer's argument well supported with evidence?

c) Has the writer given opposing viewpoints?

d) Does the writer's argument convince you?

1.4 Conclusion:

Do you feel, as the reader, that there is a suitable conclusion to the essay that refers back to the main ideas of the essay?

Task 2

Now discuss each other's drafts. Try to comment on both the strengths and weaknesses in your partner's draft.

Task 3

Consider your partner's comments carefully. Which comments do you agree with? Why? Which comments do you disagree with? Why?

Rewrite your draft, incorporating all the improvements you have discussed and considered.

PEER EVALUATION SHEET: Unit 4

ESSAY: *Statistics should be interpreted with caution as they can be misleading; they can both lie and tell the truth. Discuss.*

Task 1

Read your partner's draft carefully. Then read the following questions and reread the parts of the essay that will enable you to answer them.

1.1 Introduction:

a) Does the introduction start with a general statement related to the topic and gradually become more specific?

b) Is there a thesis statement that tells the reader what the essay will be about?

c) Does the essay explain what the thesis statement said it would?

d) What could the writer do to improve it?

1.2 Paragraphing:

a) Are the ideas in the essay grouped effectively into paragraphs?

b) If not, does the writer need to change the order of ideas?

c) Does each paragraph have a paragraph leader that tells the reader what the main idea of the paragraph is?

d) What is the function of each paragraph leader?

e) Does the writer explain enough about the main idea in each paragraph to make it clear to the reader?

f) If not, does the writer need to add further information or examples to make a point clearer?

g) Does the writer need to remove unnecessary information?

h) Does each paragraph have a concluding sentence that appropriately ends the paragraph?

i) Find two concluding sentences and write down what you think their function is.

1.3 Incorporation of sources:

a) Is information used from the text *appropriately* incorporated and paraphrased?

b) If not, what should the writer do to improve it?

c) Underline two examples where information has been incorporated from the text.

1.4 Conclusion:

a) Does the essay have an appropriate conclusion?

b) What is the particular function of the conclusion?

c) What could the writer do to improve it?

Task 2

Now discuss each other's drafts. Try to comment on both the strengths and weaknesses in your partner's draft.

Task 3

Consider your partner's comments carefully. Which comments do you agree with? Why? Which comments do you disagree with? Why?

Rewrite your draft, incorporating all the improvements you have discussed and considered.

Reading & Writing

PEER EVALUATION SHEET: Unit 5

ESSAY: *What role has human activity played in causing climate change?*

Task 1

Read your partner's draft carefully. Then read the following questions and reread the parts of the essay that will enable you to answer them.

1.1 Introduction:

a) Does the introduction start with a general statement related to the topic and gradually become more specific?

b) Is there a thesis statement that tells the reader what the essay will be about?

c) Does the essay explain what the thesis statement said it would?

d) What could the writer do to improve it?

1.2 Definitions:

a) Underline any definitions of important words or expressions that the writer has made.

b) Has the writer used appropriate language in her/his definitions?

c) If the writer has not included any definitions, do you think s/he should have? If so, what words should s/he have defined?

1.3 Paragraphing:

a) Are the ideas in the essay grouped effectively into paragraphs?

b) If not, does the writer need to change the order of ideas?

c) Does each paragraph have a paragraph leader that tells the reader what the main idea of the paragraph is?

d) What is the function of each paragraph leader?

e) Does the writer explain enough about the main idea in each paragraph to make it clear to the reader?

f) If not, does the writer need to add further information or examples to make a point clearer?

g) Does the writer need to remove unnecessary information?

h) Does each paragraph have a concluding sentence that appropriately ends the paragraph?

i) Find two concluding sentences and write down what you think their function is.

1.4 Conclusion:

a) Does the essay have an appropriate conclusion?

b) What is the particular function of the conclusion?

c) What could the writer do to improve it?

Task 2

Now discuss each other's drafts. Try to comment on both the strengths and weaknesses in your partner's draft.

Task 3

Consider your partner's comments carefully. Which comments do you agree with? Why? Which comments do you disagree with? Why?

Rewrite your draft, incorporating all the improvements you have discussed and considered.

PEER EVALUATION SHEET: Unit 6

ESSAY: *Discuss the positive and negative effects of globalization on the world today.*

Task 1

Read your partner's draft carefully. Then read the following questions and reread the parts of the essay that will enable you to answer them.

1.1 Introduction:

a) Does the introduction start with a general statement related to the topic and gradually become more specific?

b) Is there a thesis statement that says what the essay will be about?

c) Does the essay explain what the thesis statement said it would?

d) What could the writer do to improve it?

1.2 Definitions:

a) Has the writer used appropriate language in her/his definitions?

b) If the writer has not included any definitions, should s/he have? What words should s/he have defined?

1.3 Overall organization:

a) What pattern of organization has the writer used?

b) Is it clear that the writer is writing about *cause and effect*?

c) How could the writer improve her/his overall structure?

1.4 Paragraphing:

a) Are the ideas in the essay grouped effectively into paragraphs?

b) If not, does the writer need to change the order of ideas?

c) Does each paragraph have a paragraph leader that tells the reader what the main idea is?

d) Does the writer explain enough about the main idea in each paragraph to make it clear?

e) If not, does the writer need to add further information or examples?

f) Does the writer need to remove unnecessary information?

g) Does each paragraph have a concluding sentence that appropriately ends the paragraph?

1.5 Incorporation of sources:

a) Is any information used from the text *appropriately* incorporated and paraphrased?

b) If not, what should the writer do?

c) Underline two examples where information has been incorporated.

1.6 Conclusion:

a) Does the essay have an appropriate conclusion?

b) What is the particular function of the conclusion?

c) What could the writer do to improve it?

Task 2

Now discuss each other's drafts. Try to comment on both the strengths and weaknesses in your partner's draft.

Task 3

Consider your partner's comments carefully. Which comments do you agree with? Why? Which comments do you disagree with? Why?

Rewrite your draft, incorporating all the improvements you have discussed and considered.

APPENDIX 1: Questions and Glossary for Unit 4, Ex 1.7

Answer the following questions, based on the text. The glossary below may help you with any difficult words in the text.

a) What is the implication of the information introduced by the phrase *On the face of it* … (line 12)?

_____

b) What information contradicts this implication?

_____

c) What detail is causing the problem?

_____

d) What word in the last sentence of the tenth paragraph is the key word in the rise in violent crimes?

_____

e) What is the significance of the last paragraph?

_____

Glossary

remorselessly	without stopping (especially of an unpleasant situation)
fiasco	a complete and embarrasing failure
to dispel	to remove unpleasant feelings or beliefs
to soar	to increase quickly to a high level
to puncture	to cause a sudden change in viewpoint
quirk	something strange that happens for unknown reasons
a surge	a sudden increase
to transpire	to happen
to endorse	to express support for someone or something
to undermine	to make something less effective

APPENDIX 2: Organizing Essays of Comparison & Contrast

A description based on comparison and contrast can be developed in two ways:

● You can group the main ideas about Subject A in one paragraph or section and the main ideas about Subject B in the next paragraph or section, in a *vertical* movement, as in the diagram opposite:

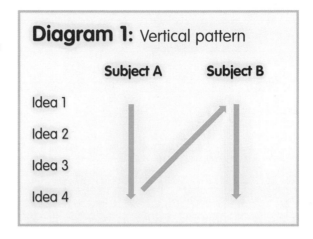

Diagram 1: Vertical pattern

Subject A   Subject B

Idea 1

Idea 2

Idea 3

Idea 4

● Alternatively, you can treat the corresponding ideas on Subject A and Subject B as a pair, and compare and contrast them one after the other in a *horizontal* movement, as in the diagram opposite:

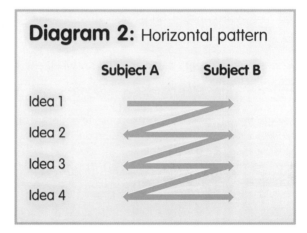

Diagram 2: Horizontal pattern

Subject A   Subject B

Idea 1

Idea 2

Idea 3

Idea 4

Whether you choose the *vertical* or the *horizontal* pattern depends on the kind of text you are writing, its purpose, and your own preference. Some writers and readers find the *horizontal* pattern clearer because it repeatedly reminds them of the comparison or contrast relationship. Others prefer the *vertical* pattern because of its relative simplicity. The *horizontal* pattern is often more suitable for a longer piece of writing. Both patterns are commonly used in descriptions involving comparison and contrast.

1.1 Does the paragraph below follow a *vertical* or *horizontal* pattern of organization?

Apples are generally oval in shape. They range in color from green to yellow to red. Their texture is usually firm and sometimes even hard. Most oranges, however, are more round in shape. Their color range is more limited—from vermillion to pale orange. In terms of texture they are relatively soft.

1.2 Rewrite the paragraph so that it follows the opposite pattern of comparison/contrast.

1.3 Now write a short paragraph comparing the food in your country with the food in another country you know. Choose either the vertical or horizontal pattern.

_____

_____

_____

_____

_____

_____

_____

_____

_____

1.4 Read another student's paragraph and say whether it is written with a horizontal or vertical pattern.

1.5 Rewrite the paragraph using the opposite pattern. There are a number of useful expressions and markers that are commonly used when comparing and contrasting. Most of them are given below.

Comparison within sentences

X is	very	like Y	in terms of	quality/size.
X and Y are	quite	similar	with respect to	expense.
X is	rather	similar to Y	with regard to	

| X resembles Y | in that | they are both large/expensive. |

X is	exactly	the same as Y.
	precisely	
	just	
	virtually	
	almost	
	nearly	

| X is costly to buy | and | it is (also) costly to maintain. |

Comparison between sentences

X is expensive to buy.	Similarly, Likewise, Moreover, Furthermore, In addition,	it is expensive to maintain/operate.

Contrast within sentences

X is unlike Y X differs from Y X and Y differ X is different from Y X contrasts with Y	with respect to with regard to in terms of in that x is smaller/more expensive, etc.	size/expense, etc.

X has four aspects,	whereas while but yet although	Y has three.

X is	considerably a great deal (very) much rather somewhat a little slightly only just scarcely	smaller than Y.

Contrast between sentences

X is expensive to buy.	However, Conversely, By/In contrast, On the other hand,	it is cheap to operate/maintain, etc.

APPENDIX 3: Assessing my Progress

In this section, you will assess the progress in your academic writing that you have made so far on this course by evaluating the essays you have written and deciding on your strengths and weaknesses.

1.1 Thinking about the input that you have had on this course on developing your academic writing, re-read your essays and the feedback that the instructor has given you; look for strengths and weaknesses that occur in more than one essay. Ask yourself these questions:

- Is the content in my essays consistently relevant and well developed?

- Do I have consistent problems with organization?

- Do I make repeated mistakes with certain language areas?

- If so, can I identify exactly which areas I need to work on?
  (e.g., agreement of subject and verb; present perfect tense)

1.2 Complete the table on page 151 with relevant comments in the appropriate columns.

1.3 What action are you going to take to ensure you continue to develop your academic writing skills?

_____

_____

_____

_____

_____

_____

_____

_____

_____

_____

_____

_____

_____

_____

_____

My Progress in Academic Writing

Name: _____

	What I've been taught and can apply in my essays	What I've been taught, but have difficulty in applying in my essays	Overall strengths	Overall weaknesses	My main areas to focus on in the future
Task achievement (relating the essay to the title or topic, and overall completion of essay)					
Organization					
Content					
Language					

Texts

FINANCE AND ECONOMICS   *The Economist*, May 12th, 2001

Economics focus:
On the move

Economic analysis sheds light on the history of immigration and on its future

1949: Passengers at Cobh Harbour, County Cork, bound for Canada. Passage cost one hundred pounds.

During the spread of globalization in the three centuries leading up to the First World War, the migration of workers was consistently one of the biggest causes of economic change. Since 1945, the world has experienced a new era of globalization which is much quicker, and the international movement of labour is proving once again to be of the greatest significance. That is so despite the efforts of governments in richer countries to restrict migration, and despite basic changes in its economic nature. As a new study* by Barry Chiswick of the University of Illinois at Chicago and Timothy Hatton of the University of Essex makes plain, it is economic factors that have been the most important throughout the history of migration.

For many years after the discovery of America, the movement of free migrants from Europe was steady but quite small: transport costs were high, conditions harsh and the dangers of migration great. In 1650, a free migrant's passage to North America cost nearly half a year's wages for a farm labourer in southern England. Indentured work developed as a way around this. This meant that the workers were forced to work for their bosses for a period of time without pay. However, direct slavery dominated until the slave trade was stopped in the first half of the 19th century. By around 1800, North America and the Caribbean Islands had received some 8m immigrants. Of these, about 7m were African slaves.

The first era of mass voluntary migration was between 1850 and 1913. Over 1m people a year were attracted to the new world by the turn of the 20th century. Growing prosperity, falling transport costs relative to wages and lower risk all

Economic analysis sheds light on the history of immigration and on its future

pushed in the same direction.

Between 1914 and 1945, war, global depression and government policy helped to reduce migration dramatically. During some years in the 1930s, people returning to Europe from the United States, even though comparatively few, actually outnumbered immigrants going the other way—a rare case for America of net emigration.

After the Second World War, the economics of migration reasserted itself. The cost of travel fell steeply. But now the pattern changed. Before long, Europe declined as a source of immigration and grew as a destination. Emigration from developing countries expanded rapidly: incomes there rose enough to make emigration feasible, but not enough to make it pointless. Many governments began trying to control immigration. The numbers of legal and illegal immigrants grew nonetheless, as economics had its way.

Winners and losers

Migration, it is safe to assume, is in the interests of (voluntary) migrants; they would not move otherwise. The evidence suggests that it is also very much in the overall interests of the receiving countries. But, as Chiswick and Hatton point out, there are losers in those countries. The increase in the supply of labour presses down the wages of competing workers, at least in the first instance. (Later, as the stock of capital grows in response, that effect may be partially reversed.)

The economic conditions now seem favourable for an enormous further expansion of migration. On the face of it, this will be much like that of a century ago. As before, the main expansionary pressures are rising incomes in the rich countries and rising incomes in the poor ones. (This second point is often neglected: as poor countries get a little less poor, emigration tends to increase, because people acquire the resources to move.) The study emphasizes, however, two crucial differences between then and now.

One is that, in the first decade of the 20th century, the receiving countries needed lots of unskilled workers in industry and farming. In the first decade of the 21st century, in contrast, opportunities for unskilled workers who can migrate are decreasing. In America, wages of unskilled workers are falling, in absolute as well as relative terms. The fall is enough to hurt the workers concerned, but not to deter new immigrants. Several studies suggest that immigration has made a definite contribution to this decline.

And the other big difference between now and a century ago? It is that the affected rich-country workers are in a stronger position to complain, and get something done. The most likely result is that a trend that is already well established (either as explicit policy or customary practice) will continue; countries will try to restrict the immigration of unskilled workers, giving preference to workers with skills.

This does help, in one way, quite apart from reducing the skills deficit in rich countries; it eases the downward pressure on wages at the bottom. However, the idea has disadvantages too. It turns away many of the poorest potential migrants, which is hard to justify in humanitarian terms. Also it pushes others from this group into illegal immigration, which exposes them to dangers, makes assimilation more difficult and may even cause a stronger downward pull on the wages of some low-skilled workers in receiving-countries than the legal entry of the same migrants.

On top of all this is the skills drain from the sending countries. Already some of the world's poorest nations lose almost all the doctors they train to jobs in Europe or North America. Financial remittances offset some of that loss, but not all.

Today's migration, much more than the migration of old, causes some insoluble problems. Regard for individual freedom argues for a more liberal immigration regime in the rich countries, and for unskilled migrants as well as skilled ones. With or without such a regime, more migrants are coming. And in either case, the question of compensation for the losers, in rich countries and poor countries alike, will demand some attention.

*Chiswick, Barry R. and Hatton, Timothy J. (August 2002) "International Migration and the Integration of Labour Markets," ftp://repec.iza.org/RePEc/Discussionpaper/dp559.pdf

Source: On the move. (2001, 12 May). [Electronic version]. *Economist, 359*(8221), 78.

THE INFLUENCE OF CLASS SIZE ON ACADEMIC ACHIEVEMENT

Education is a pillar of modern society and the subject of endless, often passionate arguments about how it can best be improved. In the U.S., there is heated debate following revelations that the country's secondary school students perform poorly relative to many Asian and European students. The news coincided with increasing concern over the nation's urban and lower-income suburban schools, too many of which are languishing at achievement levels far below those of middle-class and upper middle-class suburban schools.

Of all the ideas for improving education, few are as simple or attractive as reducing the number of pupils per teacher. With its uncomplicated appeal and lack of a big, powerful group of opponents, class-size reduction has lately developed from a subject of primarily academic interest to a key political issue. In the United States, more than 20 states and the federal government have adopted policies aimed at decreasing class sizes, and billions of dollars have been spent or committed in the past few years. The demand for smaller classes is also growing in Canada, Australia, the United Kingdom, and even Japan, whose record of secondary school performance is the envy of most other developed countries.

The most obvious drawback to class-size reduction is the huge cost. It requires more teachers, more classrooms, and more classroom equipment and resources. These expenses can dwarf the price of alternative schemes, such as testing teachers or increasing their pay as a means of attracting better candidates. The state of California, for example, has been spending more than $1.5 billion annually over the past several years to reduce class size to 20 or fewer for children in the four- to seven-year-old bracket. On the other hand, if smaller classes really do work, the economic benefits could be huge.

45 They would accrue not just from the benefits of a better-educated workforce but also from other sources, such as the avoided medical costs and sick days of a healthier, more informed populace.

50   The surge of interest in smaller classes has spurred fresh analyzes of the largest, most conclusive study to date, which took place in Tennessee in the late 1980s. At the same time, new data are flowing from 55 various initiatives, including the California program and a smaller one in Wisconsin. These results and analyzes are finally offering some tentative responses to the questions that researchers must answer before 60 legislators can come up with policies that make educational and economic sense: Do small classes in fact improve school achievement? If they do, at what age level do they accomplish the greatest good? What kind of 65 students gain the greatest benefit, and most importantly, how great is the benefit?

WHAT ARE THE BENEFITS OF SMALLER CLASS SIZES?

Educators have a multitude of explanations 70 for why smaller class sizes might be expected to improve academic performance, although frequently the ideas are anecdotal. Fewer students in the classroom seem to translate into less noise and disruptive 75 behavior from students, which not only gives the teacher more time for class work but also more freedom to engage students creatively—by, for example, dividing them into groups for specific projects. In addition, 80 smaller classes make it more likely that the teacher can give greater individual attention to struggling students. Smaller classes also allow teachers to encourage more discussion, assign more writing, and closely exam-85 ine their students' written work. In other words, much of the benefit of reduced class size may depend on whether the teachers adapt their methods to take advantage of smaller classes. Finally, some analysts 90 believe that the very youngest age group in smaller classes are more likely to develop good study habits, higher self-esteem and possibly other beneficial cognitive traits— which may very well persist for years, even 95 after the students have gone back to more normal-sized classes.

One way investigators have attempted to analyze the effects of class size is by reviewing existing data, such as records kept by the 100 U.S. Department of Education. These show that between 1969 and 1997, the average number of pupils per teacher in American public and private elementary schools fell from 25.1 to 18.3, a decline of greater than 105 27%. In secondary schools, the number also fell, from 19.7 to 14.0. Of concern, however, is the fact that despite these steep drops in pupil-teacher ratios, the improvement in academic performance was negligible. Data 110 from the National Assessment of Educational Progress—a series of tests that is the only United States-wide indicator of student knowledge in reading, mathematics, science and other subjects—show no significant 115 gains. In some specific age and subject categories, such as 17-year-olds and science, performance actually decreased slightly.

WHAT THE RECORD SHOWS

However, these findings do not necessarily 120 mean that class size makes no difference. For a variety of reasons, most researchers, including the writers, pay little attention to these figures (Figure 1). For instance, schools strive for more than just high test 125 scores; they also usually try to keep their dropout rate low. In fact, the dropout rate for students aged 16–24 fell from 15 to 11 percent over the period. Because dropouts generally come from the low end of the 130 achievement distribution, a reduction in dropout rate could be expected to pull down average test scores in the upper grades.

FIGURE 1: MILESTONE STUDIES IN CLASS SIZE

PROJECT	STATE	STUDENTS PARTICIPATING	APPROX. COST	SMALL CLASS SIZE	KEY FINDINGS
STAR 1985–89	Tennessee	10,000	$12m	13–17	Significant performance benefit of 0.2 standard deviation; larger gains for minority pupils
Class size reduction	California	1.8m	$5 billion	Less than 20	Small performance gain of about 0.05 to 0.1 standard deviation; no greater gains for minorities
SAGE	Wisconsin	64,000	£103m	12–15	Significant performance advantage of 0.2 standard deviation; larger gains for minority pupils

Another reason for discounting these data goes right to the heart of the difficulties in this field of study: it is hard to isolate the effects of class size from the myriad factors that influence student performance. The reality is that in 1995 only 68% of American students came from families with two parents in the home—down from 85% in 1970. The fraction of children who had difficulty speaking English rose from 2.8% in 1970 to 20.2% in 1995. There was some good news: the median level of education among parents increased slightly during that time period, as did the level among teachers, whose average amount of experience also went up.

Basically, demographic shifts make it very difficult to assess the effect of reductions in pupil–teacher ratios. Well-designed experiments attempt to cancel out the influence of those other factors by randomly assigning students and teachers to different class sizes and by including a large sample. Over the past 35 years, hundreds of studies and analyses of existing data have focused on class size. Most found evidence that smaller classes benefit students, particularly at the youngest level, and especially children in danger of becoming underachievers.

Unfortunately, most of these studies were poorly designed. Teacher and student assignments were rarely sufficiently random; a number of studies were simply too brief or too small, and too few had independent evaluation. The notable exception was the Tennessee study. The distinguished Harvard University statistician, Frederick Mosteller, has called it "one of the greatest experiments in education in United States history." The Student–Teacher Achievement Ratio, better known as Project STAR, was a state-sponsored, $12 million demonstration program (see Figure 1). Students entering kindergarten were randomly assigned to one of three kinds of classes: a small class of 13 to 17 children, a normal-sized class of 22 to 26 children, or a normal-sized class with both a teacher and a full-time teacher's assistant. The students remained in whatever category they had been assigned to until they had reached the third grade, after which they joined a normal classroom in the fourth. To ensure that teaching quality did not differ, teachers were randomly assigned to small and normal-sized classrooms. Few teachers received any special training for working with small classes, and there were no new curricular materials.

A CASE STUDY: SHINING STAR

After the study ended in 1989, researchers conducted dozens of analyzes of the data. One of the few points analysts agree on is that the teacher's assistants did not make any differ-
5 ence to academic performance. Researchers disagree about how long students have to be in smaller classes to get a benefit, how big that benefit is, when it becomes noticeable—in other words, the collected findings have
10 yielded no consensus on the issues of real interest to policymakers.

Jeremy Finn of the State University of New York and Charles M. Achilles of Eastern Michigan University found "an array of
15 benefits of small classes" in their review. Finn calculated that students in the small classes outperformed their counterparts in normal-sized classes by a fifth of a standard deviation, and that this sizable jump in achievement
20 generally appeared by the first grade. Best of all, this advantage seemed to persist into upper elementary levels even after students returned to larger classes. In order to appreciate how big a difference there is in terms of a fifth
25 of a standard deviation, it is necessary to compare two pupils first starting school who are as average as it is possible to be statistically. Both are in the 50th percentile, meaning that half of the other pupils perform better than
30 those two and that half perform worse. One student should be placed in a small class, and the other in a normal-sized class. After a year, the pupil in the small class will be in the 58th percentile—in other words, the student will be
35 doing better than nearly 60% of his or her peers—while the other student will still be doing better than only 50%. Finn and Achilles also found that the effect was stronger for ethnic minority students, by a factor of two

40 or three. In other words, black or Hispanic children improved by two-fifths to three-fifths of a standard deviation—a significant finding from a policy point of view, because minorities typically score about one standard deviation
45 below their peers on standard tests.

A few analysts, notably Eric Hanushek of Stanford University's Hoover Institute, criticize STAR and some of the key conclusions reached by its proponents. Hanushek agrees
50 that students can gain an initial benefit from small classes. But, he argues, the STAR data cannot be used to prove that the gains persist for years after a student has returned to normal-sized classes. If a child is still doing
55 well years later, it is hard to know how much of the performance stems from other factors, such as a supportive home. Hanushek also disagrees with an analysis indicating that the benefits of small classes accumulate—that
60 students who stay in such classes for several years widen the performance gap with their peers in large classes year by year. When he studied the four-year gains of STAR students who were in smaller classes from kindergarten
65 until they reached grade three, he did not find the gains to be larger than those logged in kindergarten. He and others have also shown that during the study, too many children migrated from the regular to the small classes,
70 probably because school personnel caved in to parental demands. Hanushek further asserts that STAR had insufficient checks to ensure good randomization of teacher and student placement in classes. These are good points,
75 but they do not really undermine the findings of STAR of a statistically significant benefit of being in a class of between 13 and 17, rather than 23, students.

The Authors: RONALD G. EHRENBERG, DOMINIC J. BREWER, ADAM GAMORAN and J. DOUGLAS WILLMS collaborated on a paper surveying studies of class size and academic performance for the May 2001 issue of *Psychological Science in the Public Interest*. Ehrenberg is the Irving M. Ives Professor of Industrial and Labor Relations and Economics at Cornell University and the author of *Tuition Rising: Why College Costs So Much* [Harvard University Press, 2000]. Brewer, who specializes in the economics of education, is the director of Rand Education, which analyzes programs and policies on education issues, and is a visiting professor of economics at the University of California, Los Angeles. Gamoran, a former Fulbright scholar, is a professor of sociology and education policy studies at the University of Wisconsin – Madison. Willms is a professor of the Canadian Research Institute for Social Policy at the University of New Brunswick.

Source: Ehrenberg, R.G., Brewer, D.J., Gamoran, A., & Willms, J.D. (2001). Does class size matter? [Electronic version]. *Scientific American, 285*(5), 78–85.

THE ASIAN PARADOX
HUGE CLASSES, HIGH SCORES

BY GLENN ZORPETTE

Study after study ranks schoolchildren in Japan and other developed Asian countries among the best in the world, particularly on standardized tests of mathematics and science. American high school students, meanwhile, have slipped somewhere below those in Greece, Lithuania, Taiwan, and Singapore in advanced mathematics and science. However, classes in Asia are large; forty students for one teacher would be normal in most of the region. In contrast, elementary school class sizes in the United States average about 24, according to the U.S. Department of Education.

The question is why Asian children do so well in such large classes. In Japan, for example, the discipline is legendary. Such discipline is not imposed by fearsome teachers, according to Catherine Lewis, an expert on the Japanese educational system and a senior researcher at Mills College. Instead, students are honored to be chosen to lead lessons, and they take turns calling the class to order, experiencing firsthand what it is like to quieten down an unruly group of students. As a result, teachers manage the class by relying on "the cumulative general power of self-reflection, rather than by punishing and rewarding," Lewis explains. Japanese teachers and students also spend much more time together—the usual year is about 40 days longer than in the United States—and more time bonding with one another at school festivals and on field trips and hikes. "There's an incredibly strong emphasis on class, group and school being meaningful entities for the children," Lewis says. Japan's prowess in academic achievement is also sustained by something it does not have: ethnic and linguistic diversity. Finally, Asian parents are far less likely than Americans to be divorced and are more likely to be involved in their children's education.

The downside of the Asian system is that the rigid national standards do not do much to foster creativity. At the same time, in Japan some children strive hard to excel partly because they become burdened early on by the fear of failing.

Given the deep cultural differences, it is not clear which parts of the Asian formula could work in other countries such as America. However, the Asian experience does demonstrate what can be done when discipline grows from the bottom up. In that kind of environment, elementary school teachers can focus on "creating happy memories," as one Japanese teacher described her main purpose to Lewis.

Glenn Zorpette is a writer based in New York.

Source: Zorpette, G. (2001). The Asian Paradox. In R.G. Ehrenberg, D.J. Brewer, A. Gamoran, & J.D.Willms, *Does class size matter?* [Electronic version]. *Scientific American, 285*(5), 78–85.

Early human development

Interaction between nature and nurture

A The question of whether heredity ("nature") or environment ("nurture") is more important in determining the course of human development has been debated through the centuries. For example, the
5 seventeenth-century British philosopher John Locke rejected the prevailing notion of his day that babies were miniature adults who arrived in the world fully equipped with abilities and knowledge and who simply had to grow in order for these inherited characteristics
10 to appear. On the contrary, Locke believed that the mind of a newborn infant is a "blank slate" (*tabula rasa*). What gets written on this slate is what the baby experiences—what he or she sees, hears, tastes, smells, and feels. According to Locke, all knowledge comes to us
15 through our senses. It is provided by experience; no knowledge or ideas are built in.

B Nineteenth-century theories emphasizing the biological basis of human development led to a return of the hereditarian viewpoint. With the
20 rise of behaviorism in the twentieth century, however, the environmentalist position once again gained dominance. Behaviorists such as John B. Watson and B.F. Skinner argued that human nature is completely malleable: early
25 training can turn a child into any kind of adult, regardless of his or her heredity. Watson stated the argument in its most extreme form: "Give me a dozen healthy infants, well-formed, and my own specified world to bring them up in,
30 and I'll guarantee to take any one at random and train him to be any type of specialist I might select—doctor, lawyer, artist, merchant-chief, and yes, beggar-man and thief, regardless of his talents, penchants, tendencies, abilities,
35 vocations, and race of his ancestors" (1930, p.104).

C Today most psychologists agree not only that both nature and nurture play important roles but that they interact continuously to guide development.
40 For example, we shall see in Chapter 12 that the development of many personality traits, such as sociability and emotional stability, appear to be influenced about equally by heredity and environment; similarly, we shall see in Chapter 15
45 that psychiatric illnesses can have both genetic and environmental determinants.

D Even development that seems most obviously to be determined by innate biological timetables can be affected by environmental events. At the
50 moment of conception, a remarkable number of personal characteristics are already determined by the genetic structure of the fertilized ovum. Our genes program our growing cells so that we develop into a person rather than a fish or
55 chimpanzee. They decide our sex, the colour of

Text 2-1: Interaction between nature and nurture cont.

Early human development

our skin, eyes, and hair and general body size, among other things. These genetic determinants are expressed in development through the process of maturation—innately determined
60 sequences of growth and change that are relatively independent of environmental events.

E For example, the human fetus develops within the mother's body according to a fairly fixed time schedule, and fetal behaviour, such as
65 turning and kicking, also follows an orderly sequence that depends on the stage of growth. However, if the uterine environment is seriously abnormal in some way, maturational processes can be disrupted. For example, if the mother
70 contracts German measles during the first three months of pregnancy (when the fetus's basic organ systems are developing according to the genetically programmed schedule), the infant may be born deaf, blind or brain-damaged,
75 depending on which organ system was in a critical stage of development at the time of infection. Maternal malnutrition, smoking, and consumption of alcohol and drugs are among the other environmental factors that can affect
80 the normal maturation of the fetus.

F Motor development after birth also illustrates the interaction between genetically programmed maturation and environmental influence. Virtually all children go through the same sequence of
85 motor behaviors in the same order: rolling over, sitting without support, standing while holding on to furniture, crawling, and then walking. But children go through the sequence at different rates, and developmental psychologists began
90 very early in the history of the discipline to ask

whether learning and experience play an important role in such differences.

G Although early studies suggested that the answer was no (McGraw, 1935/1975; Dennis & Dennis,
95 1940; Gesell & Thompson, 1929), more recent studies indicate that practice or extra stimulation can accelerate the appearance of motor behaviors to some extent. For example, newborn infants have a stepping reflex; if they are held in
100 an upright position with their feet touching a solid surface, their legs will make stepping movements that are similar to walking. A group of infants who were given stepping practice for a few minutes several times a day during the first two
105 months of life began walking five to seven weeks earlier than babies who had not had this practice (Zelazo, Zelazo & Kolb, 1972).

H The development of speech provides another example of the interaction between genetically
110 determined characteristics and experience. In the course of normal development, all human infants learn to speak, but not until they have attained a certain level of neurological development; no infant less than a year old
115 speaks in sentences. But children reared in an environment in which people talk to them and reward them for making speechlike sounds talk earlier than children who do not receive such attention. For example, children reared in
120 middle-class American homes begin to speak at about one year of age. Children reared in San Marcos, a remote village in Guatemala, have little verbal interaction with adults and do not utter their first words until they are
125 over two years old (Kagan, 1979).

Capacities
of the newborn

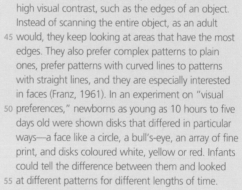

A At the end of the nineteenth century, psychologist William James suggested that the newborn child experiences the world as a "buzzing, blooming confusion," an
5 idea that was still prevalent as late as the 1960s. We now know that newborn infants enter the world with all sensory systems functioning and are well prepared to learn about their new environment.

B Because babies cannot explain what they are doing or tell us what they are thinking, developmental psychologists have had to design some very ingenious procedures to study the capacities of young infants. The basic method
15 is to introduce some change in the baby's environment and observe his or her responses. For example, an investigator might present a tone or a flashing light and then see if there is a change in heart rate or if the baby turns its
20 head or sucks more vigorously on a nipple. In some instances, the researcher will present two stimuli at the same time to determine if infants look longer at one than the other. If they do, it indicates that they can tell the stimuli apart and
25 may indicate that they prefer one to the other.

Vision

C Because the visual system is not well developed at birth, newborns have poor visual acuity, their ability to change focus is limited, and they are very
30 nearsighted. An adult with normal vision is said to have 20/20 vision; a nearsighted adult with 20/30 vision is able to see at 20 feet what an adult with normal vision can see at 30 feet. Using this same index, a newborn has 20/660 vision. At six
35 months this has improved to 20/100; and by two years, the child can see almost as well as an adult (Courage & Adams, 1990).

D Despite their visual immaturity, newborns spend a lot of time actively looking about. They scan the
40 world in an organized way and pause when their eyes encounter an object or some change in the visual field. They are particularly attracted to areas of high visual contrast, such as the edges of an object. Instead of scanning the entire object, as an adult
45 would, they keep looking at areas that have the most edges. They also prefer complex patterns to plain ones, prefer patterns with curved lines to patterns with straight lines, and they are especially interested in faces (Franz, 1961). In an experiment on "visual
50 preferences," newborns as young as 10 hours to five days old were shown disks that differed in particular ways—a face like a circle, a bull's-eye, an array of fine print, and disks coloured white, yellow or red. Infants could tell the difference between them and looked
55 at different patterns for different lengths of time.

E The possibility that there is an inborn, unlearned preference for faces initially aroused great interest, but later research showed that infants are not attracted to faces *per se* but to stimulus characteristics such as
60 curved lines, high contrast, interesting edges, movement and complexity—all of which faces possess (Banks, Salapatek, 1983; Aslin, 1987). Newborns look mostly at the outside contour of a face, but by two months they focus on the inside of the face —the
65 eyes, nose, and mouth (Haith, Bergman, & Moore, 1977). At this point parents notice with delight that the baby has begun to make eye contact.

Text 2-3: Hearing, taste, and smell

Early human development

Hearing, taste, and smell

F Newborn infants will startle at the sound of a loud noise. They will also turn their heads toward the source of a sound. Interestingly, the head-turning response disappears at about six weeks and does not reemerge until three or four months of age, at which time the infants will also search with their eyes for the source of the sound.

G The temporary disappearance of the head-turning response probably represents a maturational transition from a reflexive response controlled by subcortical areas of the brain to a voluntary attempt to locate the sound source. By four
10 months, they will reach in the correct direction toward the source of sound in the dark; by six months, they show a marked increase in their responsiveness to sounds that are accompanied by interesting sights and are able to pinpoint the
15 location of sound more precisely, an ability that continues to improve into their second year (Hillier, Hewitt & Morrongiello, 1992; Ashmead *et al.*, 1991; Field, 1987).

H Newborn infants can also detect the difference
20 between very similar sounds, such as two tones that are only one note apart on the musical scale (Bridger, 1961), and they can distinguish sounds of the human voice from other kinds of sounds. We will see in Chapter 9 that they can also
25 distinguish a number of critical characteristics of human speech. For example, one-month-old infants can tell the difference between such similar sounds as "pa" and "ba." Interestingly, infants can distinguish between some speech sounds
30 better than adults. These are sounds that adults "hear" as identical because they are not distinguished in their native language (Aslin, Pisoni & Jusczyk, 1983). By six months of age, the child will have picked up enough information about the
35 language that it will also have begun to "screen out" sounds it does not use (Kuhl *et al.*, 1992). Thus, human infants appear to be born with perceptual mechanisms already tuned to the properties of human speech that will help them
40 in their mastery of language (Eimas, 1975).

I Infants can discriminate differences in taste shortly after birth. They prefer sweet-tasting liquids to those that are salty, bitter, sour, or bland. The characteristic response of the newborn to a
45 sweet liquid is a relaxed expression resembling a slight smile, sometimes accompanied by lip-licking. A sour solution produces pursed lips and a wrinkled nose. In response to a bitter solution, the baby will open its mouth with
50 the corners turned down and stick out its tongue in what appears to be an expression of disgust.

J Newborns can also discriminate among odors. They will turn their heads toward a sweet smell,
55 and their heart rate and respiration will slow down, indicating attention. Noxious odors, such as ammonia or rotten eggs, cause them to turn their heads away; heart rate and respiration accelerate, indicating distress. Infants
60 are even able to discriminate subtle differences in smells. After nursing for only a few days, an infant will consistently turn its head toward a pad saturated with its mother's milk in preference to one saturated with another
65 mother's milk (Russell, 1976). Only breast-fed babies show this ability to recognize the mother's odor (Cernoch & Porter, 1985). When bottle-fed babies are given a choice between their familiar formula and the smell
70 of a lactating breast, they will choose the latter (Porter *et al.*, 1992). Thus, there seems to be an innate preference for the odor of breast milk. In general, the ability to distinguish among smells has a clear adaptive value:
75 it helps infants avoid noxious substances, thereby increasing their likelihood of survival.

Reading & Writing

Source: Adapted from Atkinson, R.L., Atkinson, R.C., Smith, E.E., Bem, D.J. & Nolen-Hoeksema, S. (1999). Hilgard's introduction to psychology (13th ed.). Fort Worth: Harcourt Brace College Publishers.

ENVIRONMENT **TODAY**

ACID RAIN IN NORWAY

Although some of the effects of acidic deposits from the atmosphere—so-called "acid rain"—were identified nearly 150 years ago, the problem was only recognized as an international issue in the 1960s. This was when researchers in Scandinavia suggested that much of the enhanced acidity precipitation falling there was due to the long-range transport of pollutants from other countries. Transboundary transport of pollution is now a widely accepted idea, and a number of international efforts to combat the problem have been launched. *Environment Today* in this issue looks at the situation in Norway, where the acidification of freshwater ecosystems has shown some improvement in recent years.

Damage to rivers and lakes

Sulphur dioxide (SO_2) and nitrogen oxides (NO and NO_2, collectively referred to as NO_x) have deleterious effects on many parts of the environment on which they are deposited. They have adverse effects on human health, and on the growth of green plants, in which they inhibit photosynthesis. Acid rain also damages buildings, corroding paint and metals and accelerating the weathering of some building stones. In Norway the cost of this type of damage to buildings is estimated to be NOK 200–300 million (£16–24 million) each year.

The effects of acid rain on soil and water depend upon their natural "buffering capacity"—the ability of soil and water to neutralise incoming acids. This buffering capacity is largely determined by the nature of the bedrock: ecosystems on hard, impervious igneous or metamorphic rock, with low calcium and magnesium contents, are most at risk of acidification from acid rain. All environments can withstand acid input up to a certain level—the "critical load," but beyond that level significant changes occur.

Perhaps the most notable acid rain damage in Norway has been to freshwater ecosystems. The death of fish is one of the most reliable indicators of acidification. Fish die for two main reasons. When acidification reaches a certain level, young fish fresh from the spawn cannot survive. Different species have different levels of tolerance, but the most sensitive are trout and salmon. The presence of aluminium is another common cause of fish death. Aluminium ions are washed out of soils and rocks by incoming hydrogen ions in acid rain, and aluminium is toxic to fish because it prevents them from absorbing salts and destroys their gills.

One study of 1,679 lakes in the south of the country in the 1970s found that brown trout were absent or had only sparse populations in more than half

Text 3a-1: Acid rain in Norway cont.

Figure 1: Lime used to reduce acidification damage in Norway

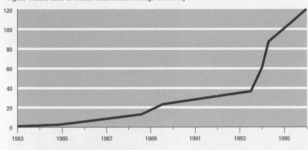

Figure 2: Emissions of sulphur dioxide in Norway

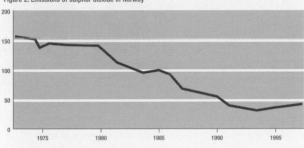

Figure 3: Emissions of nitrogen oxides in Norway

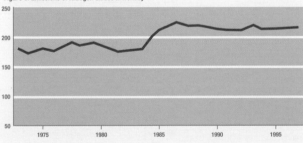

the lakes. The proportion of
90 lakes with no fish at all increased
with declining pH levels (i.e.,
increasing levels of acidity).
From 1960 to 1990, areas in
southern Norway where fish
95 stocks have been damaged have
increased fivefold.

Combating acid rain damage

These depressing statistics of
acid rain damage in Norway,
100 largely concentrated in southern
parts of the country, have generated action on a number of
fronts. One method used to deal
with the problem of acidified
105 waters in the short term is the

application of lime, to increase
pH and reduce acid levels. In
Norway, the use of lime has
increased rapidly since the early
110 1980s, and in the mid-1990s
about 120,000 tonnes were
applied (Figure 1). In 1995, lime
was applied in more than 2,500
locations, covering a precipita-
115 tion area of about 6,400 km².
However, lime can only repair
acidification damage to a certain
degree. It will never be a permanent solution.

120   In the long term, reduction
of acid rain damage can only be
achieved by reducing emissions
of acid rain compounds at their
source. To achieve these aims, a

125 number of international agreements have been reached and,
under these agreements,
Norway has made three main
political pledges:

130 ■ *to reduce sulphur dioxide emissions to 76% of the 1980 level;*
   ■ *to stabilize oxides of nitrogen
emissions at the 1987 level;*
   ■ *to reduce oxides of nitrogen*
135 *emissions to 70% of the
1986 level.*

On the sulphur dioxide front,
Norway has almost achieved its
aim already (Figure 2). Between
140 1980 and 1995, sulphur dioxide
emissions were reduced by 75%

Reading & Writing

Table 1: Excess deposits of sulpher in Norway

Year	Area where critical load exceeded (% national land area)
1985	30%
1995	25%
2010	16%

due to increased taxes on sulphur in oils and a reduction in the sulphur content of light heating oils and diesel. Efforts to reduce emissions of nitrogen oxides have not been so successful (Figure 3). After an increase in emissions of 29% from 1980 to 1987, they were reduced by 5% in the period 1987–1995, and Norway remains one of the highest emitters of nitrogen oxides in Europe when measured in per capita terms. The goal of reducing emissions to 70% of the 1986 level seems unlikely to be achieved.

However, important though the efforts in Norway are, the fact remains that most of the acid rain falling on the country is emitted by other countries. No less than 95% of the sulphur deposited on Norway, and 86% of the nitrogen compounds, is due to long-range transboundary air pollution. Emissions from Great Britain and Germany, for example, each contribute more pollution to the Norwegian environment than domestic sources. Emissions from these and other countries are, however, also being reduced. The sulphur content of precipitation falling on Norway has fallen by more than 40% since 1980, and the goals set for countries by the Sulphur Protocol of 1994 aim to reduce it still further.

The 1994 Sulphur Protocol was a milestone in international pollution control in that it was based on the critical loads approach and assigned different levels of reduction to different countries, aiming to bring about environmental improvements at the lowest possible cost. Britain, for example, has committed to an 80% reduction in emissions by the year 2010 from the baseline year of 1980, while Germany's commitment is 87%. Most countries reached their reduction targets by the year 2000, but for some the full reductions will not be reached before 2010. The benefits of these reductions for Norway are already being felt. While 30% of Norwegian territory received amounts of sulphur that exceeded the critical load in 1985, this figure has been reduced by 25% by 1990 and should be cut to 16% by 2010 (Table 1).

Although there is no doubt that the acid rain problem in Norway, and elsewhere in Europe, is being tackled, one lesson of this is clear: preventing acid rain damage and rehabilitating affected ecosystems is a long-term exercise. For some acidified lakes, researchers believe that it might take more than 100 years before fresh waters regain something close to their original species composition with stable and maintained functions.

References

- Mason, C.F. (1996), *Biology of Freshwater Pollution*, 3rd edn, Longman.
- Morecroft, M. (1995), "Air pollution and the nitrogen cycle," *Geography Review*, Vol. 9, No 2, pp. 7–10.
- Whyatt, D. and Metcalf, S. (1995), "Sulphur emissions and acid rain," *Geography Review*, Vol. 9, No 1, pp. 14–18.

by NICK MIDDLETON

Nick Middleton *is a Lecturer in Physical Geography at St. Anne's and Oriel Colleges, Oxford University. His special interests include drylands and environmental issues.*

Source: Middleton, N. (1998). Acid rain in Norway. *Geography Review, 11*(4), 6–7.

Text 3a-2: Skylarks in decline

ENVIRONMENT **TODAY**

SKYLARKS IN DECLINE

The skylark is one of Britain's commonest birds, yet its population on farmland may have fallen by nearly 60% in just over 20 years. If we are to stop this decline, and hopefully reverse it, we need to understand the underlying causes, and to study the ecology of the species.

Where do we get our facts from? Britain and Ireland can be divided into 3,862 10km x 10km squares, and data on bird distribution are held by the British Trust for Ornithology (BTO), an organization concerned primarily with long-term surveys, population work and ringing and migration studies. From time to time, distribution records of different groups are published. When *The Atlas of Breeding Birds in Britain and Ireland* was published in 1976 it revealed that the skylark was the most widespread bird in Britain and Ireland—present in 98% of the 10km squares. Skylarks were known to breed in 86% of the squares in which they were recorded and probably bred in the other 14%.

The total skylark population in Britain and Ireland in 1976 was estimated to be between two and four million pairs, on the assumption that each 10km square would hold between 500 and 1,000 breeding pairs. However, this involved some degree of informed guesswork because skylarks live in such a wide variety of open habitats with low vegetation (mainly grasslands, but also heaths, moors, salt marshes and farmland) and relatively little was known about population densities outside farmland.

During 1988–1991 there was a repeat scheme published as *The New Atlas of Breeding Birds in Britain and Ireland.*

When the number of 10km squares occupied was compared with those occupied in 1968–72, it revealed that skylarks had lost a small amount of ground—about 3%. The new scheme's more detailed work on the numbers of birds produced a more reliable estimate for the skylark population, concluding that there were about two million pairs in Britain and a further 570,000 in Ireland. It might seem that the estimate of 2.57 million pairs fits within the earlier estimate, but when we look at the part of the survey for which we have most detail, a different story emerges.

Decline on lowland farms

The only detailed evidence we have of any decline concerns skylarks on lowland farmland. We have no firm evidence for other habitats, and it is most

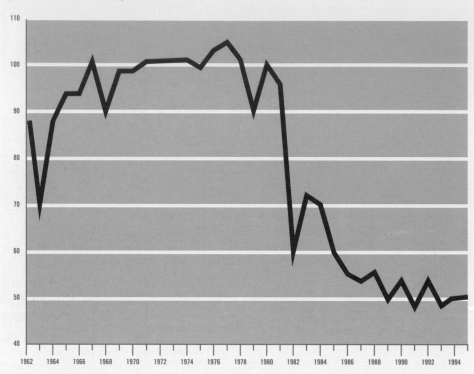

Figure 1: *Common Bird Census* indices for Skylark, 1962–1994

80 important to remember this when discussing falling skylark numbers. We know that on lowland farmland (which the *New Atlas* shows as having the
85 highest densities of breeding skylarks) the breeding population has fallen by about 58% over a 20-year period (see Figure 1). This huge decline
90 has been mirrored in other common farmland birds, including grey partridge, turtle dove, barn owl and corn bunting. The source of our
95 evidence is the BTO's long-running *Common Birds Census*. Repeated annually, the census uses a mapping technique to produce a year-by-year index
100 for all the species involved, calculated against a "reference" or "datum" year (1980) where the index is given an arbitrary value of 100. The indices pro-
105 vide a handy way of plotting the population ups and downs

of a large number of species and, importantly, of identifying longer-term trends.

110 Possible reasons for the decline

It is clear that something has gone badly wrong for farmland birds during the last 20–25 years. To find out what has hap-
115 pened to the skylark, and why, and also to investigate means of putting the situation right, the Royal Society for the Protection of Birds has begun a new
120 research programme. It is likely that what we learn about skylarks will have some relevance to other farmland species too.

Most of us only see sky-
125 larks singing high in the sky. They build a simple grass-lined nest among grass or crops, and chicks and adults feed on seeds, leaves, worms,
130 insects and larvae. There have been radical changes in agri-

cultural practices over the last 25 years and, given what is already known about skylark
135 ecology, it is reasonable to infer that these changes are implicated in its decline.

(1) Increased areas of cereals

It seems likely that the wide-
140 spread change from mixed farming regimes to monoculture has had a profound effect on skylarks. The disappearance of grass meadows may have
145 meant a reduction in insect food available for chicks, for instance. Where a variety of crops were grown, skylarks could always find suitable nest-
150 sites, and since cropping patterns and timing varied so much they could enjoy a prolonged breeding season. Cereal monocultures, on the other
155 hand, provide much less choice and are also only suitable for nesting for a very short period.

Text 3a-2: Skylarks in decline cont.

A skylark nest in a Suffolk wheatfield

Skylark feeding her young

A skylark's nightmare! Cereal crops are aiding the decline

160 This timing problem has probably been made worse by the modern practice of autumn sowing—the crops become too dense for nest sites very early in the season. Autumn sowing has also led to the virtual dis-

165 appearance of winter stubbles, which we know were very important sources of skylark food in winter. Skylarks would almost certainly fare much

170 better with more spring sowing, or at least a mixture of this and autumn sowing.

(2) Reduction of insect food by pesticides

175 Autumn sowing and the monoculture system depend on heavy applications of pesticides. A combination of insecticides and herbicides probably reduces insect

180 food supplies both for adult and young skylarks, and destroys many insect food plants. In addition, because pesticides are applied very early in the growth

185 cycle with autumn-sown cereals, it is very likely that insect food is greatly reduced by spring, when young skylarks need it most.

(2) Reduction of insect food
190 **in intensively managed pastures**

Intensively managed pastures, with high densities of grazing livestock and heavy applications of nitrogen fertilizer to maxi-

195 mize the production of good grass, are bad news for skylarks, and this is not just because more animals means a greater chance

200 of nests being trampled. The dense, uniform sward produced is not very good for nesting and carries far fewer insects than old-fashioned pastureland.

Designing a plan of action

205 We know already that skylarks fare better on mixed farmland, and also where organic farming is practised. They do very well, too, on "set-aside land," which is either

210 land put out of crop production for several years, or fields or field margins from which no crop is taken for a year. Farmers are compensated for setting land aside, and it can

215 help to reduce some persistent weeds. We have a number of ideas about how the situation could be improved for skylarks elsewhere, but we need to translate ideas and

220 intuition into a programme supported by good science. For this reason, the RSPB has embarked upon a three-year research programme, investigating skylark

225 ecology on 12 farms in three counties—four each in Norfolk, Oxfordshire and Dorset. This gives a good regional spread to the work, but it also involves three dif-

230 ferent categories of farm on predominantly arable land where cattle and sheep are reared, and in mixed farming areas.

If we are to begin to help sky-
235 larks, we must find out a great deal more about precisely what they need from a modern farming landscape. The research will tell us which habitats they feed in, both

240 in summer and in winter; exactly what adults and chicks eat; how breeding success varies on different crop types, and whether this varies from farm to farm and

245 between regions; and, hopefully, more about winter survival. In three years' time we hope that our action plan for skylark conservation will be much improved by

250 this new research input.

Further reading

■ RSPB (1996) "Crisis point," Birds, the magazine of the RSPB, Vol. 16, Issue 3, pp 17–21.
■ RSPB (1996), "The Skylark," Birds, the magazine of the RSPB, Vol. 16, Issue 3, pp 24–27.

by MIKE EVERETT

Mike Everett *works for the Royal Society for the Protection of Birds (RSPB), Europe's largest voluntary wildlife conservation organization, with one million members. The RSPB's primary function is to conserve the UK's birds and their habitats, both through the promotion of more wildlife-friendly planning and land-use policies. The Society is increasingly involved with similar work overseas and is the UK partner of the global conservation body Birdlife International. Detailed investigation of the ecology of declining and Red List bird species is an important aspect of the Society's applied research.*

Source: Everett, M. (1997). Skylarks in decline. *Biological Sciences Review,* 10(2), 7–10.

The Economist, June 7, 2008

Telemedicine comes home

Telemedicine permits remote consultations by video link and even remote surgery, but its future may lie closer to home.

Few places on earth are as isolated as Tristan da Cunha. This small huddle of volcanic islands, with a population of just 269, sits in the middle of the South Atlantic, 1,750 miles from South Africa and 2,088 miles from South America, making it the most remote settlement in the world. So it is a bad place to fall ill with an unusual disease, or suffer a serious injury. Because the islands do not have an airstrip, there is no way to evacuate a patient for emergency medical treatment, says Carel Van der Merwe, the settlement's only doctor. "The only physical contact with the outside world is a six- to seven-day ocean voyage," he says. "So whatever needs to be done, needs to be done here."

Nevertheless, the islanders have access to some of the most advanced medical facilities in the world, thanks to Project Tristan, an elaborate experiment in telemedicine. This field, which combines telecommunications and medicine, is changing as technology improves. To start with, it sought to help doctors and medical staff exchange information, for example by sending X-rays in electronic form to a specialist. That sort of thing is becoming increasingly common. "What we are starting to see now is a patient–doctor model," says Richard Bakalar, chief medical officer at IBM, a computer giant that is one of the companies in Project Tristan.

A satellite-internet connection to a 24-hour emergency medical centre in America enables Dr Van der Merwe to send digitised X-rays, electrocardiograms (ECGs) and lung-function tests to experts. He can consult specialists over a video link when he needs to. The system even enables cardiologists to test and reprogram pacemakers or implanted defibrillators from the other side of the globe. In short, when a patient in Tristan da

Telemedicine comes home

Cunha enters Dr Van der Merwe's surgery, he may as well be stepping into the University of Pittsburgh medical center. It is a great comfort to local residents, says Dr Van der Merwe, knowing that specialist consultations are available.

Most of the technology this requires is readily available, and it was surprisingly simple to set up, says Paul Grundy, a health-care expert at IBM. The biggest difficulty, he says, was to install the satellite-internet link. In theory, this sort of long-distance telemedicine could go much further. In 2001 a surgeon in New York performed a gall-bladder removal on a patient in Paris using a robotic-surgery system called Da Vinci. Although that was technologically impressive, it may not be where the field is heading.

Home is where the technology is

For advances in telemedicine are less to do with the *tele*-than with the *medicine*. In the long term, it may be less about providing long-distance care to people who are unwell, and more about monitoring people using wearable or implanted sensors in an effort to spot diseases at an early stage. The emphasis will shift from acute to chronic conditions, and from treatment to prevention. Today's stress on making medical treatment available to people in remote settings is just one way telemedicine can be used—and it is merely the tip of a very large iceberg that is floating closer and closer to home.

That is because telemedicine holds great promise within mainstream health care. Countless trials are under way to assess technology that can monitor people who have been diagnosed with heart conditions, or diseases like diabetes, from the comfort of their own homes. Rather than having their devices periodically checked at a clinic, some pacemaker patients can now have their implants inspected via mobile phone. That way, they need only visit the clinic when it is absolutely necessary.

Similarly, BodyTel, based in Germany, is one of several firms to have developed sensors based on Bluetooth wireless technology that can measure glucose levels, blood pressure, and weight, and upload the data to a secure web server. Patients can then manage and monitor their conditions, even as they give updates to their doctors. Honeywell, an American industrial giant, has devised a system that patients can use at home to measure peak flow from their lungs, ECG, oxygen saturation and blood pressure, in order to monitor conditions ranging from lung disease to congestive heart failure. Doctors continually review the data and can act, by changing the patients' medication, for example, if they spot any problems.

This sort of thing appeals to both patients and health-care providers alike. The patients keep their independence and get to stay at home, and it costs less to treat them. And as populations age in developed countries, the prospect of being able to save money by treating people at home looks increasingly attractive.

It is not just people with diagnosed conditions who are starting to receive this kind of equipment. Since 2006, Britain has spent £80m ($160m) on "preventative technology grants," which provide special equipment to enable 160,000 elderly people to stay in their homes.

Most of today's technology, however, calls on the patients to remember to monitor themselves, and also requires them to operate the equipment. For some patients, such as those in the early stages of Alzheimer's disease, that is impractical. So a lot of work is being done to automate the monitoring process and make the equipment easier to use.

William Kaiser and his colleagues at the University of California, Los Angeles, have developed a "smart cane" to help monitor and advise people convalescing at home, for example. "It has force sensors that measure pressure at the tip of the cane and around the handle. It also has motion sensors and accelerometers," says Dr Kaiser. It uses these to calculate the gait of the patient and work out how they are doing with the cane, giving them feedback about how they could make better use of it to recover from, for example, a hip replacement. "It provides guidance, either as beeps or it can talk to you," he says.

Another approach is to

The Economist, June 7, 2008

use sensors embedded in the home. Oliver Goh of Implenia, a Swiss building-management firm, has come up with a system to monitor the well-being of the occupant of a house. Using sensors on doors and mattresses, smart pill boxes that can tell when they are being opened, heart-monitors and a location-sensing wrist-watch—the system allows carers to keep tabs on elderly people. Implenia now has six elderly volunteers lined up to test the technology, says Mr Goh. He hopes that if they have a heart attack, cannot get out of bed, or need help, their carers will soon know. Ultimately, he says, the aim is to see if this sort of approach can help to extend life expectancy.

Prevention is better than cure

Looking even further ahead, some day it may make sense to give these technologies to healthy people, the "walking well." If sensors can monitor people without a threat to their privacy or comfort, doctors may be able to spot diseases before the patient notices any symptoms. "It's moving from telemedicine to telehealth and teleprevention," says Dr Grundy of IBM. It could also improve the efficiency of health-care systems, he says.

This kind of approach could save money as well as spotting illnesses early, says Dr Kaiser. "We'll detect them earlier when the cost of treatment and impact on an individual will be less," he says. The technology for this does not yet exist, admits

John Linkous, executive director of the American Telemedicine Association. "There still isn't a device that can give you a complete body check" he says. "But I'm very optimistic about it in the long run."

One idea is to use wireless infra-red skin sensors to measure blood-count, heart-rhythm and the level of oxygen in the blood. Another is to implant wireless sensors powered by the wearer's own body heat. Yet another common idea is to use smart toilets that can monitor human waste for the telltale signs of intestinal disease or cancer. The hard part is not so much developing the sensor technology, says Dr Linkous, as sifting through the results. "It would produce a tsunami of data, and the problem is that we aren't set up with health-care systems that can deal with all that," he says.

The answer will be even more technology, says Dr. Bakalar. "There has to be a way of filtering this information so that it doesn't overwhelm the medical services," he says. The obvious approach is to use "expert systems"—software programmed with expert medical knowledge and that can make clinical judgments.

Like telemedicine, expert systems have been around for some time. Trials in Denmark, to advise doctors how to prescribe, suggest the technology has great scope. Sometimes they can reach better clinical judgments than human experts do. But they are not widely used, partly because doctors are unwilling to be bossed around by a computer in the corner, but also because they have been difficult to integrate into medical practice. They could be ideally suited to telehealth, however, quietly sifting through the data generated by sensors and only raising the alarm and calling in their human colleagues when it becomes necessary to do so.

The shift from telemedicine to telehealth reflects a broader shift from diagnosis and treatment to "wellness." Taken to its technological conclusion, this would involve using wireless sensors and implants to screen entire populations for early signs of disease as they go about their daily lives. If it can be made to work, the days of making an appointment to see your doctor when you are not feeling well could be over. Instead, it may well be your doctor who calls you.

Source: Telemedicine comes home. (2008, 7 June) [Electronic version]. *Economist 387*(8583), 28–30.

STATISTICS
◆◆◆
WITHOUT TEARS

MAKING SENSE OF EXPERIENCE

It is by making sense of our experience that we human beings grow wiser and gain greater control over the environment we live in. This has been true for the development of the human race over the centuries. It is equally true for each of us as individuals in our own lifetimes. Fortunately, we
5 have this capacity for noticing things. We observe people, things, and events in the world around us. We notice their similarities and differences, their patterns and regularities—especially when such features could endanger us or, alternatively, be turned to our advantage.

Many of our observations involve us in counting and
10 measuring. Perhaps we do so in rough-and-ready fashion, and often so intuitively that we are scarcely aware of this habit of "quantification." Nevertheless our observations and comparisons are often in terms of "how much?", "how big?", "how often?", "how far?", "how difficult?", "how quickly?", "how well?", and so on.

15 Sometimes our observations concern a single thing or person or event. For example, we may notice the size of the potato crop in a particular field this year. We may make several observations about the same thing: not only the size of the crop in this field but also how much fertilizer was used, the nature of the soil, how much sunshine and rain it
20 had, etc. Sometimes our observations concern several similar but different things. For example, we may observe the size of the potato crop in several different fields this year, or in the same field over a succession of years.

Thus, we may make one or more observations on one individual, or we may do so for several individuals. Soon we have a
25 *collection* of observations (or "data," to use the technical jargon).

Inquisitively, as if by instinct, we start looking at connections and patterns, similarities and differences, among the things we happen to have noticed. We ask ourselves questions about the data.

For example, what questions might we ask in looking for connections
30 among the data we have collected about the size of potato crops?

STATISTICS WITHOUT TEARS—MAKING SENSE OF EXPERIENCE

SECTION 2

We might ask: is the size of the crop similar in all fields this year? Or, is it similar in this field from one year to another? If not, why not? What else is different about those fields, or years, that might explain the differences?

35   All such questions lead to an even more vital one: what can we learn from the connections we see among this collection of data that might help us act more effectively in the future?

This is where statistics comes in. It has been developed as a way of making sense of collections of observations. It aims, particularly,
40 to help us avoid jumping to conclusions and to be cautious about the extent to which we can *generalize* from our always limited experience.

The tendency to generalize is an essential part of our everyday thinking. Because this particular field was generously treated with a
45 certain fertilizer and gave a bigger than usual potato crop, we may feel inclined to generalize and suggest that, therefore, *other* fields so treated would give bigger than usual potato crops.

Would you think it safe to generalize in this way—on the basis of experience with one field? Why, or why not?

STATISTICS WITHOUT TEARS—MAKING SENSE OF EXPERIENCE

SECTION 3

50 In fact, such a generalization would be rather dangerous—it is very likely to be wrong. The bigger crop may be due not to the fertilizer but to, say, the weather. (That is, we may have jumped to an incorrect conclusion.) So even the same field, treated in the same way with fertilizer, may give a very different yield in another year.
55 And as for the other fields, they may differ in yet other ways that could influence the potato yield, e.g., type of soil, crop grown in the previous year, prevalence of plant disease in neighbouring fields, and so on. (Hence the weakness in our generalization.)

So, what is true of one field in one year may not be true of the
60 same field in other years, let alone of other fields. If we want to generalize more confidently, we need more experience more observations. The more fields we look at, and over more and more years, the more confident we can be in suggesting how the potato crop is likely to turn out in other, similar fields.

65 But notice the word "likely" in the sentence above. "Likelihood" or "weighing up the chances" (that is, "probability") is central to the statistical view of the world. It recognizes no 100% certainties, especially when dealing with individual people, things or events. For example, a particular kind of field may, *in general*, produce a bigger
70 potato crop if treated in a certain way, but there will be many exceptions.

In which of these two cases would you think me more likely to be proved correct:

(a) If I predict that fields of a certain type will, in general,
75 produce a bigger crop if treated in such-and-such a way? or

(b) If I predict that any such *particular* field you care to pick out will do so?

STATISTICS WITHOUT TEARS—MAKING SENSE OF EXPERIENCE

I'd be more likely to be correct in (a) than in (b). While such fields in general (maybe nine out of ten of them) will behave as expected, I
80 can't be sure that any one particular field you happen to choose will be one of those that do.

As you will learn, statistics helps us to look for reliable regularities and associations among things "in general" and "in the long run." At the same time, however, it teaches us proper caution in
85 expecting these to hold true of any particular individuals. The two chief concerns of statistics are with (1) summarizing our experience so that we and other people can understand its essential features, and (2) using the summary to make estimates or predictions about what is likely to be the case in other (perhaps future) situations.

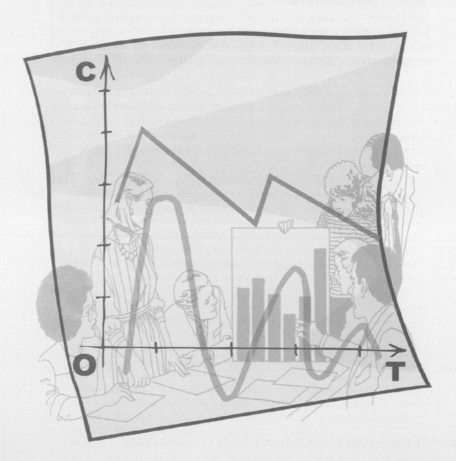

SECTION 5

WHAT IS STATISTICS?

90 Before we go any further, we'd better take note, in passing, that the word "statistics" is used in at least four different senses. First of all, it can indicate, very broadly, a whole *subject* or *discipline*, and everything that gets studied or practised in its name. Secondly, and more specifically, the term may refer to the *methods* used to collect or

95 process or interpret quantitative data. Thirdly, the term may be applied to *collections of data* gathered by those methods. And fourthly, it may refer to certain *specially calculated figures* (e.g., an average) that somehow characterize such a collection of data. Thus, to illustrate the four meanings in turn, a researcher in a firm's

100 *statistics* department may use *statistics* (statistical methods) to gather and interpret *statistics* (data) about the revenue from sales of a new detergent, and may summarize his findings by quoting the *statistics* of "average sales per thousand of population" in various towns and "range of sales revenue from town to town."

105   The meaning I shall emphasize in this book is the second of those mentioned above: statistics as a set of *methods of inquiry*. It is these methods that enable us to think statistically—a very powerful way to think—about a variety of situations that involve measurements or observations of quantities.

110   Few professional activities are untouched by statistical thinking, and most academic disciplines use it to a greater or lesser degree. Its applications in science, especially the 'biological sciences' like genetics, medicine and psychology, are both numerous and well known. But the physical sciences (e.g., meteorology, engineering,

115 and physics) also need statistical methods. And even in the humanities, the dating of ancient fragments of textile or pottery has been revolutionized by the essentially statistical technique of radio-carbon dating; while statistical methods have also been used in literary studies to help decide such questions as whether a particular

120 author wrote a certain work, or at what point in his lifetime it was written. Statistics has developed out of an aspect of our everyday thinking to become a ubiquitous tool of systematic research.

    But it is time we got down to discussing what it is about statistical thinking that can lend itself to such a variety of pursuits.

125 Statistics arises out of caution in the face of uncertainty. Statistical thinking is a way of recognizing that our observations of the world can never be totally accurate; they are always somewhat uncertain. For instance, a child we record as being four feet in height will not be exactly that—somewhere between 3 feet $11\frac{1}{2}$ inches and 4 feet $\frac{1}{2}$

STATISTICS WITHOUT TEARS—WHAT IS STATISTICS?

130 inch maybe, but not exactly four feet. And the chance of inaccuracy is even greater if we use our present observations to estimate what observations elsewhere might reveal. Thus, we might want to use our knowledge that four feet is the average height in this child's class to predict the average height in another class.

135 In such matters there can be no certainty. But statistics enables us to estimate the extent of our errors. Thus, we may express near certainty that the child's height lies within a range of four feet plus or minus half an inch; or we may calculate that the chances are ninety-nine in a hundred that the average height in another class lies 140 within two inches of four feet.

STATISTICS WITHOUT TEARS—DESCRIPTIVE AND INFERENTIAL STATISTICS

DESCRIPTIVE AND INFERENTIAL STATISTICS

You will find that statistics textbooks commonly make a distinction between (1) "descriptive statistics" (methods used to summarize or describe our observations), and (2) "inferential statistics" (using those observations as a basis for making estimates or predictions, i.e.,
145 inferences about a situation that has not yet been observed).

Look again at those three "everyday" statements I mentioned earlier. Which of them appear(s) "descriptive" and which appears "inferential", in the sense indicated above?

   (i) "On average, I cycle about 100 miles a week;"
150   **(ii)** "We can expect a lot of rain at this time of year;"
   (iii) "The earlier you start revising, the better you are
          likely to do in the exam."

STATISTICS WITHOUT TEARS—DESCRIPTIVE AND INFERENTIAL STATISTICS

SECTION 7

Statement (i) is descriptive (an attempt to summarize experience), while (ii) and (iii) go beyond what is likely to happen in 155 the future.

The distinction between descriptive and inferential statistics depends upon another: the distinction between *samples* and *populations*.

In statistical jargon, "population" does not necessarily refer to a 160 body of people. It may refer to people, but it may equally well refer to white mice, to light bulbs of a particular brand, to substandard dwellings in inner Birmingham, to meteorites, to future examination results in British secondary schools, and so on. The point is that population refers to *all* the cases or situations that the 'statistician' 165 wants his inferences or guesses or estimates to apply to. Thus, different statisticians may be making inferences about the learning ability of (all) white mice; predicting how long all light bulbs of a particular type are likely to burn; estimating the cost of renovating (all) substandard dwellings; predicting the composition of (all) 170 meteorites; guessing the (total) numbers of candidates passing various examinations, and so on.

Perhaps it is also worth pointing out that the researcher will not be interested in every aspect of members of a population. Rather, he is interested in just some—maybe only one—of the many attributes 175 or characteristics that members might have in common. Thus a psychologist may not be concerned to speculate about the tail-length or litter-size of white mice (though these characteristics might interest other researchers); he is interested simply in their learning ability. Neither might the astrophysicist be interested in predicting 180 the geographical distribution or the size of falling meteorites as well as their composition.

However, even if he is interested in only one characteristic of his population, the researcher will be most likely to study all members of it. Usually he has to do the best he can with a SAMPLE—a relatively small 185 selection—from within the population. Often he must do this to save time and expense. For the astrophysicist to tour the world inspecting every meteorite that has ever been known to fall would be prohibitively expensive. Again, an industrial researcher who is estimating the burning-life of a brand of light bulb by 'testing to 190 destruction' cannot test all the population or there will be none left to sell.

In some cases, it may be logically impossible to study all members of the population. The population may be infinite, or simply not yet available for study. Thus, the psychologist who is studying learning 195 ability in white mice will hope his results, and therefore his inferences,

STATISTICS WITHOUT TEARS—DESCRIPTIVE AND INFERENTIAL STATISTICS

will have some application to all white mice—not just the millions that exist at this moment but also the further millions not yet born. He may even hope his results can be generalized to explain *human* learning. Likewise, the astrophysicist may well use his statistics to generalize not
200 just about the meteorites that have already fallen to earth, or even about those that will fall in future; he may hope to speculate also about the composition of other objects flying around in space.

All such researchers go *beyond* the available information. They generalize from a sample to a population, from the seen to the
205 unseen. (So do we all, though often in a rather careless, uncontrolled way, when using everyday "common sense.") This idea of generalizing from a sample applies to research in the arts as well as in the sciences. For example, one would not have to have read everything ever written by, say, D.H. Lawrence and Joseph Conrad
210 before one could begin generalizing about how they compared and contrasted as novelists. One could work from a sample of two or three books by each author.

Anyway, *descriptive* statistics is concerned with summarizing or describing a sample. *Inferential* statistics is concerned with generalizing
215 from a sample, to make estimates and inferences about a wider population. Consider a biologist experimenting with the feeding of chicks. He may report (using descriptive statistics) that particular samples of 60 chicks, fed a particular compound, grow faster than a similar sample fed on some standard diet. So much (the weight gain) he
220 reports as fact. But he goes beyond fact. He uses inferential statistics to suggest that *all* similar chicks (the wider population) would grow faster if given similar treatment.

How safe are such generalizations from a part to a whole? Well, that is largely what statistics is about: quantifying the probability of
225 error. We will be looking at the underlying ideas in subsequent chapters. One thing we can say at this stage, however: the reliability of the generalization will depend on how well the sample mirrors the population—in other words: is the sample truly representative of the population?

Source: Rowntree, D. (1982). *Statistics without tears: a primer for non-mathematicians.* Harmondsworth: Penguin.

COMMON QUESTIONS ABOUT
CLIMATE CHANGE

• United Nations Environment Programme •
• World Meteorological Organization •

The scientists listed below have volunteered their time to write and review this brochure. The brochure is co-sponsored by the United Nations Environment Programme and the World Meteorological Organization. In addition, the United Nations Environment Programme, the National Oceanic and Atmospheric Administration, the U.S. Global Change Research Program and the Rockefeller Brothers Fund contributed funds for the layout and printing of the brochure. Leonie Haimson and Christine Ennis assisted in editing and Elizabeth C. Johnston and Julianne Snider designed the layout of the brochure.

AUTHORS

- Steven R. Hamburg
  Brown University, USA
- Neil Harris
  European Ozone Research Coordinating Unit, UK
- Jill Jaeger
  International Institute for Applied Systems Analysis, Austria
- Thomas R. Karl
  National Oceanic and Atmospheric Administration, USA
- Mack McFarland
  *United Nations Environment Programme
  (on loan from the DuPont Company), Kenya*
- John R. B. Mitchell
  Hadley Centre for Climate Prediction & Research, UK
- Michael Oppenheimer
  Environmental Defense Fund, USA
- Benjamin D. Santer
  Lawrence Livermore National Laboratory, USA
- Stephen Schneider
  Stanford University, USA
- Kevin E. Trenberth
  National Center for Atmospheric Research, USA
- Tom M.L. Wigley
  National Center for Atmospheric Research, USA

REVIEWERS/CONTRIBUTORS

- Daniel L. Albritton
  National Oceanic and Atmospheric Administration, USA
- Bert Bolin
  Chairman of the Intergovernmental Panel on Climate Change, Sweden
- Theresa Cookro
  National Oceanic and Atmospheric Administration, USA
- Susana B. Diaz
  Ozone and UV Laboratory, CADIC/CONICET, Argentina

- Robert E. Dickinson
  University of Arizona, USA
- Christine A. Ennis
  National Oceanic and Atmospheric Administration, USA
- Paul J. Fraser
  Commonwealth Scientific and Industrial Research Organization, Australia
- Hartmut Grassl
  World Meteorological Organization, Switzerland
- Ann Henderson-Sellers
  Royal Melbourne Institute of Technology, Australia
- John Houghton
  Co-Chair, Intergovernmental Panel on Climate Change Working Group II, UK
- Phil Jones
  University of East Anglia, UK
- Igor L. Karol
  Main Geophysical Observatory, Russia
- Murari Lal
  Indian Institute of Technology, India
- Jerry D. Mahlman
  National Oceanic and Atmospheric Administration, USA
- Pim Martens
  University of Limburg, The Netherlands
- Mario J. Molina
  Massachusetts Institute of Technology, USA
- Henning Rodhe
  University of Stockholm, Sweden
- Keith P. Shine
  University of Reading, UK
- Peter E.O. Usher
  United Nations Environment Programme, Kenya

This document answers some of the most commonly asked questions about the impact of human activity on climate change.
www.gcrio.org/ipcc/qa/contributors.html

COMMON QUESTIONS
ABOUT CLIMATE CHANGE

A   This document answers some of the most commonly asked questions about climate change, including whether the Earth has warmed, which human activities are contributing to climate change, what further climatic changes are expected to occur, and what effects these changes may have on humans and the environment.
5   First, however, several issues have to be clarified: what the Earth's climate is, how climate differs from weather, and what processes influence climate.

B   Climate is the average weather, including seasonal extremes and variations, either locally, regionally, or across the globe. In any one location, weather can change very rapidly from day to day and from year to year, even within an unchanging climate.
10   These changes involve shifts in, for example, temperatures, precipitation, winds, and clouds. In contrast to weather, climate is generally influenced by slow changes in features like the ocean, the land, the orbit of the Earth about the sun, and the energy output of the sun.

C   Fundamentally, climate is controlled by the long-term balance of energy of the
15   Earth and its atmosphere. Incoming radiation from the sun, mainly in the form of visible light, is absorbed at the Earth's surface and in the atmosphere above. On average, absorbed radiation is balanced by the amount of energy returned to space in the form of infrared 'heat' radiation. Greenhouse gases such as water vapour and carbon dioxide, as well as clouds and small particles (called 'aerosols'), trap some
20   heat in the lower part of the Earth's atmosphere. This is called the greenhouse effect. If there was no natural greenhouse effect, the average surface temperature would be about 34°C (61°F) colder than it is today.

D   Winds and ocean currents redistribute heat over the surface of the Earth. The evaporation of surface water and its subsequent condensation and precipitation in
25   the atmosphere redistribute heat between the Earth's surface and the atmosphere, and between different parts of the atmosphere.

E   Natural events cause changes in climate. For example, large volcanic eruptions put tiny particles in the atmosphere that block sunlight, resulting in a surface cooling of a few years' duration. Variations in ocean currents change distribution of heat and
30   precipitation. El Niño events (periodic warming of the central and eastern tropical Pacific Ocean) typically last one to two years and change weather patterns around the world, causing heavy rains in some places and droughts in others. Over longer time spans, tens or hundreds of thousands of years, natural changes in the geographical distribution of energy received from the sun and the amounts of greenhouse gases and
35   dust in the atmosphere have caused the climate to shift from ice ages to relatively warmer periods, such as the one we are currently experiencing.

F   Human activities can also change the climate. The atmospheric amounts of many greenhouse gases are increasing, especially that of carbon dioxide, which has increased by 30% over the last 200 years, primarily as a result of changes in land use
40   (e.g., deforestation) and of burning coal, oil, and natural gas (e.g., in automobiles, industry, and electricity generation). If current trends in emissions were to continue, the amount of carbon dioxide in the atmosphere would double during the 21ˢᵗ century,

with further increases thereafter. The amounts of several other greenhouse gases would increase substantially as well.

G 45   The accumulation of greenhouse gases in the atmosphere due to human activities will change the climate by enhancing the natural greenhouse effect, leading to an increase in the Earth's average surface temperature. This warming may be partially offset in certain regions where air pollution leads to high concentrations of small particles in the atmosphere that block sunlight.

H 50   The current best estimate of the expected rise of globally averaged surface temperature relative to 1991 is 1 to 3.5°C (about 2 to 6°F) by the year 2100, with continued increases thereafter. Because most greenhouse gases remain in the atmosphere for a long period of time, even if emissions from human activities were to stop immediately, effects of past emissions would persist for centuries.

I 55   The Intergovernmental Panel on Climate Change (IPCC), co-sponsored by the United Nations Environment Programme and the World Meteorological Organization and made up of over 2,000 scientific and technical experts from around the world, published its First Assessment Report in 1990 and its Second Assessment Report in 1996. The Second Report contains over 10,000 references and is over 2,000 pages in 60 length. Although our understanding of some details of climate change is still evolving, the IPCC report is the most comprehensive and scientifically authoritative account of our understanding of climate change, the potential impact on humans and the natural environment, the technology currently available to reduce human influences on climate, and the socio-economic implications of possible measures to mitigate these 65 changes. The document that follows has been written and reviewed by scientists who participated in the IPCC process, and it attempts to answer some of the most commonly asked questions about these issues, based upon information contained in the IPCC reports. A list of the scientists who prepared this document is provided inside the front cover.

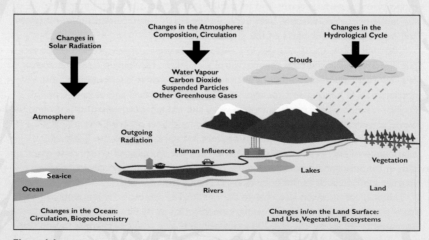

Figure 1.1

Schematic view of components of the global climate system, some of their processes and interactions, and some aspects that can cause climate change.

ARE HUMAN ACTIVITIES
CONTRIBUTING TO CLIMATE CHANGE?

A   A comprehensive assessment by the IPCC of the scientific evidence suggests that human activities are contributing to climate change, and that there has been a discernible human influence on global climate.

B   Climate changes caused by human activities, most importantly the burning of
5 fossil fuels (coal, oil, and natural gas) and deforestation, are superimposed on, and to some extent masked by, natural climate fluctuations. Natural changes in climate result from interactions such as those between the atmosphere and ocean, referred to as internal factors, and from external causes, such as variations in the sun's energy output and in the amount of material injected into the upper atmosphere by
10 explosive volcanic eruptions.

C   Studies that aim to identify human influences on climate attempt to separate a human-caused climate-change factor (the signal) from the background noise of natural climate variability. Such investigations usually consist of two parts: detection of an unusual change, and attribution of all or part of that change to a particular cause or causes.

D   15   The concepts of detection and attribution may be understood in terms of a simple medical analogy. Measurement of a body temperature of 40°C (104°F) detects the presence of some abnormal condition or symptom, but does not in itself give the cause of the symptom. To attribute the symptom to an underlying cause often requires additional and more complex tests, such as chemical analyzes
20 of blood and urine, or even X-rays and CAT scans.

E   Early work on climate change detection examined changes in the globally-averaged surface temperature of the Earth over the last century. Most studies of this type concluded that the observed increase of roughly 0.5°C (about 1°F) was larger than would be expected as a result of natural climate variability alone.

F   25   Observed globally-averaged temperature changes have also been analyzed away from the Earth's surface. The observations used come from conventional weather observing instruments (radiosondes) and from satellites. As expected, because of the different factors affecting the variability of and persistence of temperatures at different altitudes, there are noticeable differences between short-term trends at
30 the surface and those at higher altitudes. The record of temperatures away from the Earth's surface, which spans only the past 40 years compared with the much longer surface record, is too short for globally-averaged values to provide any definitive information about the extent of human influences.

G   The further step of attributing some part of observed temperature changes to
35 human influences makes use of climate models, which have been employed to estimate the climatic effects of a range of human-induced and natural factors. The human factors include recent changes in the atmospheric concentrations of both greenhouse gases and sulphate particles (called 'aerosols'). The natural factors include solar variability, the effects of volcanic eruptions, and internal variability of the climate system resulting
40 from interactions among its individual components.

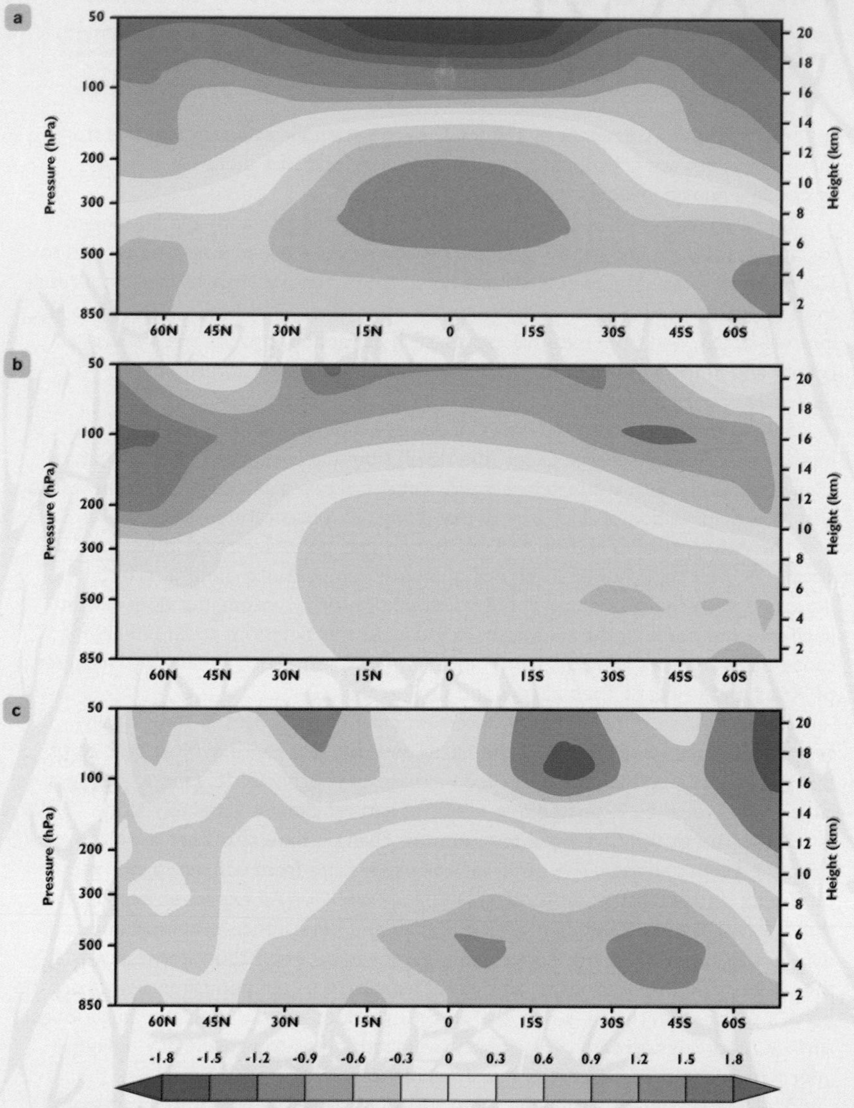

Figure 2.1

Modelled and observed changes in atmospheric temperature, from close to the Earth's surface to the lower stratosphere. Model results are from two sets of experiments: with "present-day" levels of atmospheric carbon dioxide (panel a), and with present-day carbon dioxide, sulphur emissions, and stratospheric ozone depletion (panel b). They are given as changes relative to a pre-industrial state of the atmosphere. Observed changes (panel c) are temperature trends over the period 1963 to 1988, as estimated from weather balloons. All results are for annually averaged data and are in units of degrees Celsius (panels a, b) and degrees Celsius/25 years (panel c). The patterns of change in panels b and c are similar.

H   The changes in globally averaged temperature that have occurred at the Earth's surface over the past century are similar in size and timing to those predicted by models that take into account the combined influences of human factors and solar variability.

I   To probe the question of attribution requires the application of more powerful
45 and complex methods, beyond the use of global averages alone. New studies have focused on comparing maps or patterns of temperature change in observations and in models. Pattern analysis is the climatological equivalent of the more comprehensive tests in the medical analogy mentioned previously, and makes it possible to achieve more definitive attribution of observed climate changes to a
50 particular cause or causes.

J   The expected influence of human activities is thought to be much more complex than uniform warming over the entire surface of the Earth and over the whole seasonal cycle. Patterns of change over space and time therefore provide a more powerful analysis technique. The basic idea underlying pattern-based approaches is
55 that different potential causes of climate change have different characteristic patterns of climate response or fingerprints. Attribution studies seek to obtain a fingerprint match between the patterns of climate change predicted by models and those actually observed.

K   Comparisons between observed patterns of temperature change and those
60 predicted by models have now been made at the Earth's surface and in vertical sections through the atmosphere (Figure 2.1). Model predictions show increasing agreement with changes observed over the past 30–50 years. The closest agreement occurs when the combined effects of greenhouse gases and sulphate aerosol particles are considered. Statistical analyses have shown that these correspondences are highly
65 unlikely to have occurred by chance.

L   The agreements between the patterns of change predicted by models and those actually observed are due to similarities at large spatial scales, such as contrasts between the temperature changes in the northern and southern hemispheres or between different levels of the atmosphere. It is at these large scales that we have
70 most confidence in model performance. More importantly, many of the results of these studies agree with our physical understanding of the climate system, and do not depend solely on numerical models or statistical techniques.

M   There are still uncertainties in these detection and attribution studies. These are due primarily to our imperfect knowledge of the true climate-change signal
75 due to human activities, to our incomplete understanding of the background noise of natural climatic variability against which this signal must be detected, and to inadequacies in the observational record. Such uncertainties make it difficult to determine the exact size of the human contribution to climate change. Nevertheless, the most recent assessment of the science suggests that human
80 activities have led to a discernible influence on global climate and that these activities will have an increasing influence on future climate.

WHAT HUMAN ACTIVITIES
CONTRIBUTE TO CLIMATE CHANGE

The burning of coal, oil, and natural gas, as well as deforestation and various agricultural and industrial practices, are altering the composition of the atmosphere and contributing to climate change. These human activities have led to increased atmospheric concentrations of a number of greenhouse gases, including carbon
5 dioxide, methane, nitrous oxide, chlorofluorocarbons, and ozone in the lower atmosphere. The importance of these gases is shown in Figure 3.1.

Carbon dioxide is produced when coal, oil, and natural gas (fossil fuels) are burned to produce energy used for transportation, manufacturing, heating, cooling, electricity generation, and other applications (see Figure 3.2). The use of fossil fuel currently
10 accounts for 80 to 85% of the carbon dioxide being added to the atmosphere.

Land use changes, e.g., clearing land for logging, ranching, and agriculture, also lead to carbon dioxide emissions. Vegetation contains carbon that is released as carbon dioxide when the vegetation decays or burns. Normally, lost vegetation would be replaced by regrowth with little or no net emission of carbon dioxide. However,
15 over the past several hundred years, deforestation and other land use changes in many countries have contributed substantially to atmospheric carbon dioxide increases. Although deforestation is still occurring in some parts of the northern hemisphere, on the whole, regrowth of vegetation in the north appears to be taking some carbon dioxide out of the atmosphere. Most of the net carbon dioxide
20 emissions from deforestation are currently occurring in tropical regions. Land use changes are responsible for 15 to 20% of current carbon dioxide emissions.

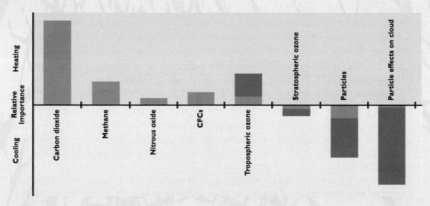

Figure 3.1
Relative importance of the various greenhouse gases and small particles currently in the atmosphere. Bars extending above the horizontal line indicate a warming effect. Bars extending below the horizontal line indicate a cooling effect. The impacts of tropospheric ozone, stratospheric ozone, and particles are quite uncertain. The range of possible effects for these gases is indicated by the bar on the darker shading; i.e., the effect is in the range of one end of the darker shading to the other.

Text 5-4: What human activities contribute to climate change cont.

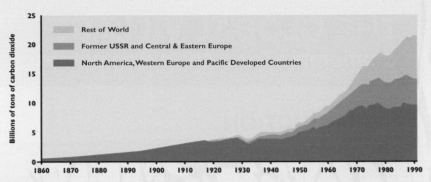

Figure 3.2

Carbon dioxide emissions from the burning of coal, oil, and natural gas are shown for the period 1860 to 1995 for three groups of countries.

Methane (natural gas) is the second most important of the greenhouse gases resulting from human activities. It is produced by rice cultivation, cattle and sheep ranching, and by decaying material in landfills. Methane is emitted during coal mining and
25 oil drilling, and by leaky gas pipelines. Human activities have increased the concentration of methane in the atmosphere by about 145% above what would be present naturally.

Nitrous oxide is produced by various agricultural and industrial practices. Human activities have increased the concentration of nitrous oxide in the atmosphere by about 15% above what would be present naturally.

30 Chlorofluorocarbons (CFCs) have been used in refrigeration, air conditioning, and as solvents. However, the production of these gases is being eliminated under existing international agreements because they deplete the stratospheric ozone layer. Other fluorocarbons that are also greenhouse gases are being used as substitutes for CFCs in some applications, for example in refrigeration and air conditioning. Although currently
35 very small, their contributions to climate change are expected to rise.

Ozone in the troposphere, that is, in the lower part of the atmosphere, is another important greenhouse gas resulting from industrial activities. It is created naturally and also by reactions in the atmosphere involving gases resulting from human activities, including nitrogen oxides from motor vehicles and power plants. Based on current
40 data, tropospheric ozone is an important contributor to the enhanced greenhouse effect. However, in part because ozone is also produced naturally, and because of its relatively short atmospheric lifetime, the magnitude of this contribution is uncertain.

Contrary to popular perception, the Antarctic ozone hole does not cause global warming. Instead, the global depletion of stratospheric ozone caused by CFCs and
45 other gases has resulted in a small cooling effect as shown in Figure 3.1.

Human activities, such as the burning of fossil fuels and changes in land use, have increased the abundance of small particles in the atmosphere. These particles can change the amount of energy that is absorbed and reflected by the atmosphere. They are also believed to modify the properties of clouds, changing the amount of
50 energy that they absorb and reflect. Intensive studies of the climatic effects of these particles began only recently and the overall effect is uncertain. It is likely that the net effect of these small particles is to cool the climate and to partially offset the warming of increasing concentrations of greenhouse gases.

Source: United Nations Environment Programme – World Meteorological Organization (1997, last modified May 24, 2006). Common questions about climate change. Retrieved January 15, 2009, from the U.S. Global Change Research Information Office web site: http://www.gcrio.org/ipcc/qa/index.htm

Reading & Writing

THE GLOBAL VILLAGE:
Challenges for a shrinking planet

INTRODUCTION

Since the Canadian academic Marshall McLuhan coined the phrase "global village" in 1969, home computers, cable television, satellite-linked mobile phones and the Internet have been added to the array of new technologies drawing the peoples of the world
5 together. But McLuhan also pointed out that the tribal-global village is not "the place to find ideal peace and harmony." Village conditions bring into focus the myriad differences between people and cultures.

Multinationals seeking to exploit the potential of economic
10 globalization are often advised to "think global, act local." While the idea of a single global purchasing culture may appeal to big business, the reality is that people's buying habits are determined as much by culture as by income—and cultures vary greatly from place to place. What sells well in Japan may stay on the shelves in
15 Canada. While some products appear to have global appeal, selling methods and local specifications may vary considerably. Even in the European Union, where trading and political ties are especially strong, there are major differences in customer behaviour. Advertising which works for Italians may turn off Scandinavians.
20 The German consumer products market is different from that in neighbouring France. This multiplicity in buying patterns extends to many other aspects of daily life—politics, food, hobbies, education and sexual relations. Even with a single country, diversity is often more apparent than homogeneity. Lager louts
25 who like to create mayhem in the streets of Paris may share a plane home with culture vultures on an art appreciation tour. Every city is a mishmash of humanity of all shades, habits and opinions. On a global scale, this variety is almost infinite.

It is sometimes argued that developments in transport and
30 telecommunications, along with the collapse of communism, have resulted in the "deaths" of distance, geography and history. In other words, people share the same view of the world whichever continent they inhabit. They are joined together by a desire to enjoy freedom, material comfort, and security. Television and the Internet
35 have created new links between people worldwide. Sport, fashion and entertainment have become global industries. Political

cooperation between nations, especially in Europe but also in intergovernmental forums in Latin America, East Asia and Africa, is much greater than it was before World War II. For all its
40 weaknesses, the UN system provides an extraordinary concentration of intergovernmental debate and cooperation. The growth of trade, tourism and foreign investment strengthens the bonds between countries and should make them less likely to fight each other. Conversely, any country which gets left out of the global system or
45 feels threatened by it, may be tempted to lash out. Hence concerns over, for example, North Korea or Iraq.

In terms of economic management, the World Bank model (based on western thinking) is used almost everywhere. Yet opinions differ strongly on the effectiveness of "structural adjustment
50 programmes" and the mix of private/public control over economic activity. The Asian financial crisis may throw up more resistance to the idea of aping the US model of society, flawed by urban deprivation and violent crime. The "global village" is perhaps closest in the financial world, where London, Tokyo, New York and about
55 20 other cities dominate a 24-hour global trading system for stocks, bonds, currencies, commodities and financial derivatives. In this screen-based village, vast sums are transferred back and forth in deals which are mostly speculative rather than directly connected to trade in merchandise or services. This "virtual" economy can have a huge
60 impact on real lives in every part of the world. The power and global reach of the money men causes unease among both peoples and governments. While poorer countries feel exposed to economic domination by the West, the growing business habit of "outsourcing" (i.e., exporting jobs) creates new tensions in richer
65 nations, where public concern over the environment has also increased. The World Trade Organisation (WTO) regulates trade but does not address the social or ecological consequences of global business activity—a shortcoming which many feel must be urgently addressed.
70 The disengagement of the global financial system from the real economy is a worrying development, especially in the light of potential penetration by organized crime. The problem with this and other aspects of globalization is that there are no effective global authorities to control it. Nations are very reluctant to share
75 sovereignty with other countries, so the move towards effective supranational institutions is slow. The US, which did so much to create the UN system in the 1940s, has become increasingly laggard in this respect. Unfortunately, the global village lacks an effective police force.

THE SHRINKING PLANET

Telecommunications and transportation systems have weakened the barriers of geography which separate different peoples. Yet many cultural differences persist.

Global communications—global understanding?

5　In 1995, according to the International Telecommunication Union (ITU), there were 211 TV sets for every 1,000 people in the world. Even in sub-Saharan Africa there were 43 sets per thousand people. Few cultural groups are so isolated that they
10　don't know how their fellow humans live. But this knowledge can increase discontent as well as cultural convergence. According to *Time* magazine, the 1998 football World Cup accumulated a total TV audience of 37 billion people—more than six times the global population.
15　Brazil's young star Ronaldo became one of the best-known people in the world. Similar fame has been accorded to media "stars" as diverse as President Clinton, Arnold Schwarzenegger and the Pope.

For most of human history, the picture of the world which most people had was determined by their immediate surroundings. There was no way of
20　knowing what was happening on the other side of the planet—other than from the stories and artefacts brought back by a few sailors, explorers or merchants.

　　The 20th century has seen a profound change. Not only has the population exploded (from 2 billion in 1930 to about 6 billion now), but technology has enabled tribesmen in Central Africa or Borneo to watch TV programmes
25　about life in New York or Paris; throngs of tourists visit the most remote corners of the globe, bringing with them new ideas, customs and languages; aboriginal groups have learned to use the Internet to publicise their grievances at the encroachment of alien modern cultures which threaten tribal traditions; books written in Germany or Canada are routinely printed in Spain or Hong
30　Kong; components of motor cars designed in Japan may be made in a dozen different countries before being assembled in Mexico or Poland; people in Korea or Tanzania may share admiration for Manchester United, Michael Jackson, Ronaldo or Princess Diana; wearing jeans, eating burgers and listening to rock music have become the daily habit of youngsters across the globe.
35　　　Yet such apparently universal links may be more superficial than they seem. An Iranian youth cannot easily shake off the Islamic culture in which he grew up. While Shanghai teenagers may appear to have more in common with their counterparts in Los Angeles than with the older generation in other oriental cities, they remain distinctly Chinese, affected by their national culture, history and
40　language. Just as it is possible for an individual to be a "good European" as well as a proud Scotsman, so fellow citizens of the "global village" can share many tastes and yet be as different from each other as chalk from cheese.

　　Sharing common interests and buying similar products do not obliterate human peculiarities. Indeed, the homogenising effect of globalization is partly

45 offset by computer technology which allows for easy customisation of products. A "world car" may have the same "platform," but is sold with different shapes, colours and accessories to meet local requirements. Ownership of global media is highly concentrated, but communication is being fragmented as digital technology enables hundreds of TV channels to be beamed to different
50 audiences with their own viewing tastes and receiving languages.

ECONOMIC GLOBALIZATION

Money is increasingly stateless, with most countries abandoning exchange controls. Businesses of all sizes can now operate on a global basis.

The global marketplace

5 Money and goods are moved from country to country with little regard for distances or borders. More and more services are traded internationally. On the other hand, labour remains largely immobile (and therefore vulnerable to job losses)—an anomaly which can have
10 serious social implications. The growth in international trade is a telling indicator of the globalization of business in recent decades. Between 1900 and 1950, world trade barely doubled. Since then, the volume of trade has risen twelvefold. In OECD countries, the
15 majority of goods used by households and industries include imported materials or parts. Complex manufacturing activities now span the globe.

A Perhaps the most obvious sign of globalization is in the economic area. The logos of corporate giants such as Coca-Cola, Nike, Shell and Mercedes are a
20 common sight in cities on every continent. While trade has long been a part of the international scene, its volume has rocketed in the last decade, along with foreign capital investment. Business operates in a worldwide environment, with competition in faraway countries as much of a threat to a manufacturer or service provider as a rival in a neighbouring town.

B 25 In 1996, foreign direct investment (FDI) around the world was $553 billion —more than twice the figure for 1990 ($239 billion). The biggest recipient countries were the US ($77 billion), China ($40 billion), the UK ($32 billion) and France ($22 billion), followed by Brazil ($10 billion), Singapore ($9 billion), Indonesia, the Netherlands and Mexico ($8 billion each), and Australia, Canada
30 and Spain ($6 billion each). Some $15 billion was invested in the former Soviet bloc in Europe and Central Asia. Elsewhere in the developing world, Malaysia, Peru, India, Argentina, Chile, Colombia, Thailand, Venezuela, Vietnam, the Philippines and Nigeria all had FDI exceeding $1 billion. Meanwhile, global merchandise exports grew from $1.9 trillion in 1980 to $5.4 trillion in 1996.

35 Trade in services has leapt ahead too. For example, it has become commonplace for European airlines to get their computer programming done in Asia and for banks, accountants and advertising agencies to sell their services in dozens of different countries.

C Services and intellectual property rights are now covered by the
40 international rules of the World Trade Organization, making it easier and more lucrative for companies to sell services and know-how across borders. Trade in goods has been encouraged by the fall in tariff barriers brought about by successive GATT[1] rounds. The weighted mean tariff for products entering the European Union was down to 5% by 1997 and just over 4% in the US. The
45 comparative figure for Japan was less than 3%. India's weighted mean tariff fell from 83% in 1990 to 27.7% in 1997 as it gradually opened itself to international trade and investment.

D Of course, tariffs do not tell the whole story, since trade can equally be impeded by cultural differences, domestic regulation, language barriers and, as
50 the World Bank delicately puts it, "private collusive behaviour and information asymmetries."

E The three most powerful trading blocs are the EU, APEC and NAFTA, which together account for over 90% of international trade. Economic globalization is a phenomenon which impacts on all countries but which is of
55 main benefit to the industrialised world—which has goods to sell and money to buy. Africa, the "lost continent," has increased its trade with the outside world but its share of global FDI and trade is tiny.

F One of the dangers of economic globalization is the further concentration of power in those who are already rich. The gap between rich and poor
60 nations has widened in recent years, despite the catch-up success of a few countries such as the Asian "tigers." A similar division is taking place between individual haves and have-nots even within the industrialised countries. Those without money are pushed to the margins of society, while commercial thinking spreads from business to penetrate socio-cultural sectors such as
65 education, health care, the arts and even religion.

G Globalization, as driven largely by short-term economic pressures, is based on consumerism, with people being regarded primarily as "customers." They are segmented by income group rather than by cultural differences. The value of, say, social manners or communal worship tends to be submerged, along with "non-
70 economic" considerations such as animal rights or the "health" of the oceans.

H Yet the image of global business as a juggernaut destroying everything in its path is misleading. Companies may try to shape consumer demand but cannot disregard customer concerns such as health and environment. The more sophisticated companies take care to emphasize their social responsibilities,
75 working more closely with governments and NGOs to ensure that "sustainability" is built into their long-term business plans. For example, Unilever's support for the Marine Stewardship Council shows how economic power can be used to protect global resources.

---

1 After 1947, rules for international trade were negotiated by member states in the General Agreement on Tariffs and Trade (GATT—the US congress having rejected the idea of an international trade organization as part of the original UN system. For over 40 years, the GATT remained a provisional set of international trading rules rather than a regulatory authority as such. The last round of GATT negotiations, known as the Uruguay Round, was completed in 1994. It greatly extended the range of trade covered and finally established the World Trade Organization, based in Geneva, to act as a global regulatory authority.

Competition and protection

80 The pressures of global competition may tempt some countries to protect their own workers from job losses by increasing trade barriers. Advocates of free trade argue that such policies result in a vicious circle of retaliatory action—and point to the protectionist, war-provoking 1930s as a grim example.

85 *The increase in global trade means that exchange rate fluctuations now play a major role in determining business success or failure. Even the best-managed company can be destroyed by a sudden move in the exchange rates. For example, businesses in Japan had to contend with a fall in the exchange rate of the yen*
90 *from 111 to the US dollar in mid-1970 to 147 in August 1998. During the same period, the Indonesian rupiah fell from 2,500 to 14,000.*

The supermarket has replaced the corner shop as the symbol of household consumerism in the global village. In
95 the West, the contents of a typical house contain products from every corner of the globe. Supermarket shelves are stacked with food brought from dozens of countries. In a pre-industrial village, what was available was largely determined by what could be grown on surrounding farms.
100 No such limitations exist in the global village.

Global financial markets

Financial services in the global village are heavily concentrated in a few OECD countries. For example, the world's stock markets carried a market capitalisation value of $20,178 billion in 1997, with the US accounting for 42% of this vast sum. The
105 leading stock markets (measured by the capital value of all stocks listed in 1997) were:

	$ billion
US	8,484
Japan	3,089
UK	1,740
Germany	671
China (inc. HK)	656
France	591

Note that US stock market capitalisation grew from $3,059 billion in 1990, while Japan's total barely increased from its 1990 level. Market
110 capitalisation of the Hong Kong exchange rose from $83 billion in 1990 to $450 billion in 1996, China's from $2 billion to $206 billion.

In mid-1998, the Frankfurt and London stock exchanges announced that they planned to
115 develop a joint electronic trading platform. Other European exchanges may decide to join later, raising the prospect of a single European stock exchange—though Paris initially reacted to the Anglo-German plan by proposing its own combination of exchanges. The large OECD countries dominate global banking, and trade in foreign exchange, commodity futures, stocks and shares, and financial "derivatives." Global derivatives contracts were valued at $55.5 trillion
120 in 1995. The combined weight of these money markets, whose activity (including daily turnover of $1.2 trillion in foreign exchange) is largely speculative—as opposed to being driven by merchandise trade ($5 trillion a year)—dwarfs global GNP ($27.8 trillion). This situation has led some commentators to describe the global financial system as "casino capitalism" which has spun out of control and threatens the "real economy." Electronic funds transfers have greatly
125 increased the difficulty of controlling (and taxing) flows of money from country to country.

Whereas the World Trade Organization provides a global regulatory body for international trade in goods and services, there is no equivalent body for the regulation of global money markets.

COMMUNITY & CONFLICT

Citizens of the global village tend to be the better educated and more prosperous of the world's people. It is a new minority group, surrounded by the poor.

A
There is no inherent conflict between being a good global citizen and being a
5 proud member of a particular regional or ethnic group, nation state or city. The same person may regard himself as a "European" or an "African" while endorsing the universal brotherhood of man. Such multi-layering of identities is common. Humans long to be part of a group, while insisting on their individuality. The habit of treating a different tribe as the enemy may be accompanied by great
10 hospitality towards strangers. Awareness of the planet's fragility may have brought moves towards the globalization of human society, but the propensity to violent conflict seems as well-honed as ever. If global war now seems unlikely, civil wars still rage worldwide.

Global village—global inequality

15 There is little sign that the economic benefits of the global village will be evenly distributed. The income gap between rich and poor has widened over the last 50 years. The technology gap has yawned wider still.

B
Ethnic divisions have not vanished but may gradually diminish under the influence of globalization. Coke and Pepsi show their customers as smiling multi-
20 ethnic crowds, implying that the world is already united in its love of soft drinks. Teenagers have their own global culture based on fashion, pop music, sports heroes and clothes. Sport is both unifying and polarising in its effect, with supporters cheering their own team and jeering their opponents.

C
More and more countries are becoming multi-ethnic, embracing large
25 numbers of foreigners. Though this creates tensions at first, the longer-term trend appears to be greater acceptance of multi-cultural society. Urbanization, another global phenomenon, has accelerated this trend, for it is easier to introduce new cultures in the relative anonymity of the city than it is in tradition-bound rural villages. In OECD countries almost 80% of the
30 population live in towns—compared to 31% in China and 27% in India. In global terms, the majority of people (54%) still live in rural areas. Yet rapid urbanization is a common feature of almost every developing country. New ideas and fashions—and diseases—spread fast in cities. In major urban centres of even the poorest countries there is a core of privileged people with access
35 to computers, mobile phones, electric razors, imported wines and other trappings of the global village.

D
A century ago agriculture employed over half the workforce even in rapidly industrializing countries. Today the global average is still over 45%. But in the UK and USA, farm workers now make up less than 3% of the workforce. Some
40 experts have suggested that a similar contraction is happening in manufacturing,

as technology enables more products to be made by computer-controlled machines. Services already account for 70% of employment in the USA. Since agriculture and manufacturing have provided the bulk of employment for hundreds of years, the transition to a radically different pattern of employment is
45 bound to be difficult. Blaming the loss of jobs on globalization is a typical reaction, with foreigners bearing the brunt of labour force discontent.

E In 1995, Germany's population included over 7 million foreigners (compared with the UK's 2 million). Germany received 788,000 immigrants in 1995. In Australia, foreign-born workers make up 24% of the total labour force. The US
50 has about 25 million foreign-born residents, accounting for about 9% of the workforce. There was a legal inflow of 721,000 in 1995 (compared with 1.5 million in 1990). Illegal immigrants probably number at least a million a year. Foreigners make up 19% of the Swiss population and 9% of the population in Austria and Belgium. The Middle East is home to large numbers of immigrant
55 workers from Egypt, Pakistan, Bangladesh and the Philippines. Workers from Bolivia and Paraguay go to Argentina in search of a better life, just as Turks go to Germany, Mexicans to the US and Algerians to France.

F Whether the world is more prone to conflict than it used to be is hard to say. Perhaps we are just more aware of violent confrontation in different parts of the
60 world. A famine in remote Sudan gets media coverage whereas a century ago starving populations might die unseen. Today's wars can be watched live on television, like Hollywood action movies. Greater awareness of the human consequences of battle may reduce the lust for war—or make it another spectator sport.

65 ### Fringe groups everywhere

The proliferation of nationalist militia groups in the US—there are over 400 groups with paramilitary training sites in over 20 states—is but one sign of the fragmentation of modern society. Hundreds of
70 other fringe groups and "eccentric" individuals have been strengthened by the ability to link with others through television and over the Internet. Thus behaviour which was once regarded as bizarre or anti-social, is increasingly regarded as a
75 "normal" part of the multi-cultural society.

G Computer-mediated communication (CMC) is being used in more and more countries as a way to enhance democracy. Over 200 cities worldwide have civic networking projects experimenting in information access and citizens' feedback and even voting. However, CMC is also used by less
80 desirable groups such as paedophile rings, gun salesmen, pornographers and political extremists. For example, the Thule-Netz in Germany provides an Internet-based information exchange which has different levels of access—to ensure that only genuine right-wing activists know what is being planned. Use of the World Wide Web gets round the problem of Germany's domestic ban on
85 the distribution of Nazi propaganda.

H   This example highlights a more general problem—how to enforce national law in the global village. Laws enacted to protect the people and environment of one country are increasingly undermined by new "global" technology (e.g., electronic funds transfer) or by international agreements (e.g., greenhouse gas 90 emissions) which tend to use a "lowest common denominator" approach in order to get consent from as many nations as possible. Organized crime has been particularly adept at exploiting the weaknesses in global law enforcement, growing at a much faster rate than most legitimate businesses. Organized crime is a major beneficiary of the global village.

95 **Cultural diversity**

Cultural diversity is one of the glories of human civilization. For example, Chiapas Indians, using caricature blond wigs and pale-faced masks, adapted Spanish cultural imports to their own use after the invasion by Cortes in the 16th century. Similarly, Western cultural exports of the late 20th century (and early 21st century) are being 100 adapted in different ways in different parts of the world. Gunpowder and disease overthrew native societies in the colonial era. Television, mobile phones and soft drinks may do the same for traditional societies in the 21st century. A major complaint of today's Chiapas-based Zapatistas movement in Mexico is the damage done to native cultures by global capitalism and the exclusion of the masses from the 105 benefits which globalization is supposed to bring.

THE SHARING OF SOVEREIGNTY

There is more and more cooperation—and even pooled sovereignty—between states. Every country is strongly influenced by external factors beyond its control.

It is sometimes argued that globalization is breaking down the system of nation 5 states upon which international relations has largely depended. Just as families once combined into tribes and tribes into nations, so nations are combining into regional power blocs, and thence perhaps to a single world political community. Such an outcome is a very long way off, but there is certainly far more cooperation between nations than there was 50 years ago. Indeed, there is 10 now a vast network of international organizations, at both government and non-government levels, bringing people together to work on the practical issues of living together in harmony.

    While nation states remain the chief building blocks of the global system, they are by no means the only players on the scene. Chief among international 15 organizations is the United Nations—much maligned for its inability to solve the world's most intractable problems (civil war, poverty, etc.) yet an essential tool for the prevention of global anarchy. In fact, the UN has provided an invaluable

forum for the exchange of views and has provided the main coordinating centre to deal with mundane but vital rules to ensure that international mail gets
20 delivered, that aircraft can fly across borders in safety, that food and industrial goods meet specificd health and safety standards. These daily achievements of UN agencies go unreported, while failures of peace-making get much media attention.

Bearing in mind the pressures on competing nations, it is perhaps
25 surprising that any major decisions can be made on a joint basis. That the European Union was able to agree (in 1986) on a majority voting system to advance the single market was an extraordinary development in international relations. The EU has gone even further along this path with the agreement by 11 of its 15 member states to pursue economic and monetary union, including
30 the use of a single currency. In the EU, at least, national sovereignty over economic matters has been pooled among 11 governments.

The United Nations

The United Nations organization provides the nearest thing to a world
35 government. Though its impact is minimal in resolving serious political conflicts, the UN has many valuable functions in smoothing international relations.

The UN is a kind of diplomatic
40 global village, which brings together thousands of government officials from 185 member countries. Their primary aim is the preservation of world peace—though UN work
45 extends to many other objectives. The UN General Assembly, comprising delegates from all UN member states, is more representative of the world community than the 15-nation Security
50 Council, but has far less power. General Assembly resolutions, even when passed with overwhelming majorities, do not bind the Security Council, which is dominated by the
55 "permanent five"—the US, China, Russia, France and the UK.

Other bodies which tie Europe's nations closer together include the European Free Trade Association, the Western European Union, the Council of Europe and the Organization for Security and Cooperation in Europe. NATO
60 provides a military alliance which links the US and Canada with Europe, and talks in the top-level "Transatlantic Business Dialogue" envisage a free trade area embracing both the European Union and North America.

International law

Most law is based on national legislation, but there is a steady accretion of international law. The UN has secured over 300 international treaties since 1945. Most countries have agreed to overriding global laws dealing with such matters as offshore territorial rights, marine pollution, international trade and nuclear proliferation. EU directives take precedence over the national laws of 15 European countries.

Shared sovereignty

The European Union provides the world's most prominent example of shared sovereignty. Since 1957, the EU has been engaged in an ambitious programme for "ever closer union among the peoples of Europe." Eleven of the 15 member states have agreed to a common economic and monetary policy, including the use of a single currency, the euro. Though efforts to develop a common approach to foreign policy have so far failed, most of Western Europe has become a closely integrated economic area, with strong political ties. The Social Chapter lays down broad principles for employee rights, while the EU has led the world in many areas of environmental law. The world's two other main trading blocs, NAFTA and APEC, are not remotely like the EU in terms of political integration and have few of the EU's supranational rules on social and environmental protection.

Even the superpower US has relinquished some of its sovereignty by, for example, joining the World Trade Organization and agreeing to abide by its rules. It will be interesting to see how often the WTO's dispute settlement procedures are called into play over the next decade and whether major economic powers can be made to toe the line, even when it hurts their domestic business interests.

American support is vital if multinational institutions are to work. Yet the US opposed the 1997 Ottawa treaty on landmines and the mid-1998 UN decision to establish an International Criminal Court. Getting out of step with global opinion will damage US security options in the long run.

CONVERGING OR DIVERGING?

Tourism, transport and telecommunications have brought the world closer together, but new cultures are being created as fast as the old ones disappear.

Since 1945 there has been an underlying assumption that the world's poorer
5 countries are gradually "developing" towards the western model and that
international aid policy should be geared to this end. The success of some
Asian countries, notably Japan (which was restructured under US guidance
after 1945), lent weight to this thesis. Though the World Bank now divides
countries into high, middle and low income countries, rather than developed
10 and developing countries, the basic premise has remained—countries afflicted
with high levels of poverty, disease and deprivation can improve their standards
by adopting western-style institutions and economic management.
   The governing elites of almost all states have come to accept that free markets,
combined with strict monetary discipline, offer the best path to improving living
15 standards. Country after country has adopted a World Bank-driven "structural
adjustment programme" in an effort to achieve economic success. The orthodox
view is that public ownership and protected markets are less efficient than private
ownership and free trade. Governments around the globe, encouraged by the
World Bank, have been busy privatising state-owned companies in everything from
20 electricity generation and telecommunications to railways and even prisons. The
notion of "public service," whether in health care or broadcasting, has given way
to "private enterprise."
   Average living standards, life expectancy and educational norms have risen
strongly in dozens of countries since 1945, though the gap between rich and
25 poor countries is wider than ever. Very few 'developing' states have managed to
catch up on the wealthy "establishment" in North America and Western
Europe. Most of the exceptions are in Asia, recently subject to financial
meltdown. "Development" has gone into reverse in Indonesia, and even Japan
and South Korea are suffering hardship. In other parts of the world, catching up
30 has been more dream than reality, at least for the vast bulk of the population.
Latin America, notorious for its uneven distribution of wealth, has had buoyant
stock markets, along with mass poverty. Living conditions in the former Soviet
Union have deteriorated for the majority while a few get very rich. Africa has
scarcely begun to improve the economic lot of its black population. If there is
35 any global pattern to all this, it seems to be that elites everywhere are doing
very well, while "ordinary people" are facing insecurity and hardship—hardly a
major departure from historical precedent. Many people, in both the
industrialised and developing worlds, feel that globalization threatens their jobs,
indeed their whole way of life.
40   There seems to be no way to insulate a modern economy from the forces
of global capitalism, yet unease about the direction such forces are taking
humanity is by no means confined to Muslims worried about western "moral
corruption," or Buddhists forsaking the material world. Islamist Iran has tried

The excluded society

45 Poverty and ignorance rule out full
participation in the global high-tech
economy for much of the world's
population. Their exclusion could be a
source of growing instability.

50 "Excluded" from the global consumer
society by poverty, Peruvian children know
as little about "information technology" as
they do about how their Inca ancestors
were able, without the use of machinery, to

55 build walls from massive but perfectly-fitted
stone blocks. Power over information and
invention has always been confined to elites.
Ownership of modern technology is heavily
concentrated in a few OECD countries. Yet

60 computers have given ordinary citizens
access to more information about
technology and government than has ever
been available before. Optimists argue that
the result will be better education, more

65 opportunity and stronger democracy.

Cultural invasions

Tourist visits worldwide more than
doubled between 1980 and 1996,
reaching almost 600 million. Television

70 and branded products reach almost
every part of the globe. But the way
that local populations react to such
"cultural invasions" varies greatly.

Networked computers

75 dramatically increase the power of
information exchange worldwide—
for scientific purposes (accelerating
invention), for social and political
activism (gathering like-minded

80 individuals) and for business
(identifying and selling into new
markets). A key characteristic of the
Internet is its chaotic diversity. With
the advent of digital television, giving

85 viewers hundreds (possibly thousands)
of channels to choose from, "chaotic
diversity" may soon overtake television
too—though standardised products are
more profitable and media ownership

90 is highly concentrated.

to resist foreign influence, but the weakness of its economy has persuaded it to adopt a more open attitude. In recent years India has also turned away from self-sufficiency to more integration with the world economy. Even North Korea, facing severe food shortages and economic decline, is keen to attract
95 foreign investment.

Tourism has made the retention of traditional cultures more difficult while giving it new economic value—thus local festivals and tribal dances are mounted not as part of regional tradition but as a show for foreign visitors. The Czech Republic (population 10 million) had 17 million tourists in 1996. Most went to
100 Prague, transforming that city from the quiet shabbiness of the communist era to the bustling "fast-food" commercialism of today. Such developments appear to reinforce the view that the world is being reshaped according to American values.

Of course, tourism is not just an American phenomenon. Germans, Britons, Japanese, Malaysians and many other nationalities travel abroad in very large
105 numbers. The total of overseas tourist visits was close to 600 million in 1996. Cheap air travel has made mass tourism possible, even to the most exotic places. The influx of tourists with different cultural values creates tensions in the receiving community—which may be suppressed when the economic benefit is sufficiently large but may rankle beneath the surface. Yet the local youths who
110 treat foreign visitors with a mixture of envy and contempt may well enjoy listening to rock music and smoking Marlboro cigarettes. They may dream of driving a BMW and having a mobile phone. Their families probably have a Japanese television set. In terms of "brand allegiance," some global convergence has already taken place. Coca-Cola is an obvious example.
115 Global broadcasting has even greater impact on popular culture, as was shown by the extraordinary worldwide attention given to the death of Princess Diana (overshadowing the death of Mother Theresa). Watching global news coverage, TV soaps and sporting events is an experience shared by billions. Yet the advent of multi-channel broadcasting will enable viewers to customise their
120 viewing habits. In short, two trends are discernible—a global convergence of certain consumption patterns, combined with a vigorous interest in localised cultures—old and new. Diversity is still the main attribute of the global village.

Source: Buckley, R. (Ed.). (1998). The global village: challenges for a shrinking planet. *Understanding Global Issues, 98*(7).

THE NEW LINGUISTIC ORDER

A As you read this sentence, you are one of approximately 1.6 billion people—nearly one-third of the world's population—who will use English in some form today. Although English is the mother tongue of only 380 million people, it is the language of the lion's share of the world's books, academic papers, newspapers,
5 and magazines. American radio, television, and blockbuster films export English-language pop culture worldwide. More than 80 percent of the content posted on the Internet is in English, even though an estimated 44 percent of online users speak another language at home. Not surprisingly, both the global supply of and the demand for English instruction are exploding. Whether we
10 consider English a "killer language" or not, whether we regard its spread as benign globalization or linguistic imperialism, its expansive reach is undeniable and, for the time being, unstoppable. Never before in human history has one language been spoken (let alone semi-spoken) so widely and by so many.

B With unprecedented reach comes a form of unprecedented power. Although
15 language is synonymous with neither ideology nor national interest, English's role as the medium for everything from high-stakes diplomacy to air traffic control confers certain advantages on those who speak it. Predominantly English-speaking countries account for approximately 40 percent of the world's gross domestic product. More and more companies worldwide are making
20 English competency a prerequisite for promotions or appointments. The success of politicians around the world also increasingly depends on their facility in English. When newly elected German chancellor Gerhard Schroeder and French president Jacques Chirac met in September to discuss future cooperation, they spoke neither French nor German, but English. And English
25 is the official language of the European Central Bank, despite the fact that the United Kingdom has not joined the European Monetary Union, the bank is located in Frankfurt, and only 10 percent of the bank's staff are British. The predominance of English has become such a sore point within the European Union that its leadership now provides incentives for staff members to learn
30 any other official language.

C Yet professional linguists hesitate to predict far into the future the further globalization of English. Historically, languages have risen and fallen with the military, economic, cultural, or religious powers that supported them. Beyond the ebb and flow of history, there are other reasons to believe that the English
35 language will eventually wane in influence. For one, English actually reaches and is then utilized by only a small and atypically fortunate minority. Furthermore, the kinds of interactions identified with globalization, from trade to communications, have also encouraged regionalization and with it the spread of regional languages. Arabic, Chinese, Hindi, Spanish, and a handful of other
40 regional tongues already command a significant reach—and their major growth is still ahead. Finally, the spread of English and these regional languages collectively—not to mention the sweeping forces driving them—have created a squeeze effect on small communities, producing pockets of anxious localization and local-language revival resistant to global change.

THE NEW LINGUISTIC ORDER

LOVE THY NEIGHBOR'S LANGUAGE

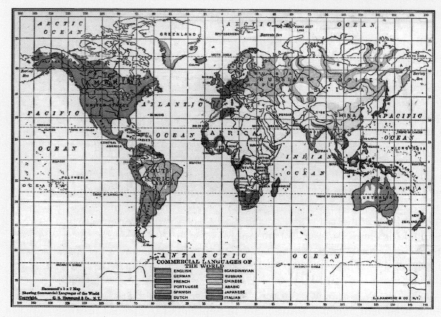

A map, post-World War I, showing the different languages spoken in different countries.

D English came to Massachusetts the same way it did to Mumbai: on a British ship. For all the talk of Microsoft and Disney, the vast reach of English owes its origins to centuries of successful colonization by England. Of the 100 colonies that achieved independence between 1940 and 1990, 56 were former British colonies, and one was an American possession. Almost every colony that won its
50 independence from England either kept English as an official language or at least recognized its utility.

E The continued spread of English today is both a consequence of and a contributor to globalization. Some factors are obvious: the growth in international trade and multinational corporations; the ever-widening reach of
55 American mass media; the expanding electronic network created by the Internet; and the linguistic impact of American songs, dress, food, sports, and recreation. Other factors are perhaps less visible but no less powerful, such as the growth in the study of English overseas and the swelling number of students who go abroad to study in English-speaking countries. In 1992, almost half of the
60 world's million-plus population of foreign students were enrolled at institutions in six English mother-tongue countries: Australia, Canada, Ireland, New Zealand, the United Kingdom, and the United States.

English for academic study

52

F Yet globalization has done little to change the reality that, regardless of location, the spread of English is closely linked to social class, age, gender, and
65 profession. Just because a wide array of young people around the world may be able to sing along to a new Madonna song does not mean that they can hold a rudimentary conversation in English, or even understand what Madonna is saying. The brief formal educational contact that most learners have with English is too scant to produce lasting literacy, fluency, or even comprehension.
70 Indeed, for all the enthusiasm and vitriol generated by grand-scale globalization, it is the growth in regional interactions—trade, travel, the spread of religions, interethnic marriages—that touches the widest array of local populations. These interactions promote the spread of regional languages.

G Consider the case of Africa, where some 2,000 of the modern world's approximately
75 6,000 languages are spoken and 13 percent of the world's population lives. English is neither the only nor even the best means to navigate this linguistic obstacle course. Throughout East Africa, Swahili is typically the first language that two strangers attempt upon meeting. The average East African encounters Swahili in a variety of contexts, from the market, elementary education, and government
80 "how to" publications, to popular radio programming and films. New movies from India are often dubbed in Swahili and shown in towns and villages throughout Kenya, Tanzania, and Uganda. In West Africa, some 25 million people speak Hausa natively and perhaps double that number speak it as a second or third language, due in large part to burgeoning regional business at local markets
85 throughout the region. Since most Hausa speakers are Muslim, many of them also attend Koranic schools where they learn Arabic, itself a major regional language in North Africa. Thus, many Africans are trilingual on a functional basis: local mother tongues among "their own," Hausa for trade and secular literacy, and Arabic for prayer and Koranic study. Hausa speakers firmly believe that Hausa
90 has great prospects as a unifying language for even more of West Africa than it already reaches. Its main competition will not likely come from English but rather from other regional languages such as Woloff—which is also spreading in markets in and around Senegal—and Pidgin English.

H Increased regional communication, informal market interaction, and migration
95 are driving regional language spread around the world just as they are in Africa. Mandarin Chinese is spreading throughout China and in some of its southern neighbors. Spanish is spreading in the Americas. Hundreds of varieties of Pidgin English have emerged informally among diverse groups in Australia, the Caribbean, Papua New Guinea, and West Africa. The use of French is still
100 increasing in many former French colonies, albeit much more slowly than at its peak of colonial influence. Hindi is reaching new learners in multilingual, multiethnic India. And Arabic is spreading in North Africa and Southeast Asia both as the language of Islam and as an important language of regional trade.

I Some languages are spreading in part due to the efforts of organizations and
105 government committees. France spends billions of francs annually to support

French-language conferences, schools, and media that promote French as a
vehicle for a common French culture. Muslim organizations in the Middle East
spread knowledge about Islam worldwide with an extensive array of English
pamphlets and other literature, but they cultivate their ties with each other in
110 Arabic. Moreover, in promoting Islam within their borders, many governments
seek to Arabize local ethnic minorities (for example, Berbers in Morocco and
Christians in Sudan). The German government funds 78 Goethe Institutes,
scattered from Beirut to Jakarta, that offer regular German language courses as
well as German plays, art exhibits, lectures, and film festivals. Singapore, a tiny
115 country with four official languages, is in the nineteenth year of its national
"Speak Mandarin" campaign. Singapore designed the campaign to encourage
dialect-speaking Chinese to adopt a common language and facilitate the use of
Mandarin as a regional tongue.

J The importance of regional languages should increase in the near future. Popular
120 writers, itinerant merchants, bazaar marketers, literacy advocates, relief workers,
filmmakers, and missionaries all tend to bank on regional lingua francas whenever
there is an opportunity to reach larger, even if less affluent, populations. In many
developing areas, regional languages facilitate agricultural, industrial, and
commercial expansion across local cultural and governmental boundaries. They
125 also foster literacy and formal adult or even elementary education in highly
multilingual areas. Wherever the local vernaculars are just too many to handle,
regional languages come to the fore.

HOME IS WHERE THE TONGUE IS

K For all the pressures and rewards of regionalization and globalization, local
identities remain the most ingrained. Even if the end result of globalization is to
130 make the world smaller, its scope seems to foster the need for more intimate
local connections among many individuals. As Bernard Poignant, mayor of the
town of Quimper in Brittany, told the *Washington Post*, "Man is a fragile animal
and he needs his close attachments. The more open the world becomes, the more
ties there will be to one's roots and one's land."

L In most communities, local languages such as Poignant's Breton serve a strong
symbolic function as a clear mark of "authenticity." The sum total of a community's
shared historical experience, authenticity reflects a perceived line from a culturally
idealized past to the present, carried by the language and traditions associated
(sometimes dubiously) with the community's origins. A concern for authenticity
140 leads most secular Israelis to champion Hebrew among themselves while also
acquiring English and even Arabic. The same obsession with authenticity drives
Hasidic Jews in Israel or the Diaspora to champion Yiddish while also learning
Hebrew and English. In each case, authenticity amounts to a central core of

THE NEW LINGUISTIC ORDER

cultural beliefs and interpretations that are not only resistant to globalization but
145 are actually reinforced by the "threat" that globalization seems to present to these
historical values. Scholars may argue that cultural identities change over time in
response to specific reward systems. But locals often resist such explanations and
defend authenticity and local mother tongues against the perceived threat of
globalization with near religious ardor.

M As a result, never before in history have there been as many standardized languages
as there are today: roughly 1,200. Many smaller languages, even those with far
fewer than one million speakers, have benefited from state-sponsored or voluntary
preservation movements. On the most informal level, communities in Alaska and
the American northwest have formed Internet discussion groups in an attempt to
155 pass on Native American languages to younger generations. In the Basque, Catalan,
and Galician regions of Spain, such movements are fiercely political and frequently
involve staunch resistance to the Spanish government over political and linguistic
rights. Projects have ranged from a campaign to print Spanish money in the four
official languages of the state to the creation of language immersion nursery and
160 primary schools. Zapatistas in Mexico are championing the revival of Mayan
languages in an equally political campaign for local autonomy.

N In addition to invoking the subjective importance of local roots, proponents of local
languages defend their continued use on pragmatic grounds. Local tongues foster
higher levels of school success, higher degrees of participation in local government,
165 more informed citizenship, and better knowledge of one's own culture, history, and
faith. Navajo children in Rough Rock, Arizona, who were schooled initially in
Navajo, were found to have higher reading competency in English than those who
were first schooled in English. Governments and relief agencies can also use local
languages to spread information about industrial and agricultural techniques as
170 well as modern health care to diverse audiences. Development workers in West
Africa, for example, have found that the best way to teach the vast number of
farmers with little or no formal education how to sow and rotate crops for higher
yields is in these local tongues. From Asturian to Zulu, the world's practical
reliance on local languages today is every bit as great as the identity roles these
175 languages fulfil. Nevertheless, both regionalization and globalization require that
more and more speakers and readers of local languages be multiliterate.

LOOKING AHEAD

O Since all larger language communities have opted to maintain their own
languages in the face of globalization, it should come as no surprise that many
smaller ones have pursued the same goal. If Germans can pursue globalization
180 and yet remain German-speaking among themselves, why should Telagus in
India not aspire to the same?

THE NEW LINGUISTIC ORDER

P Multilingualism allows a people this choice. Each language in a multilingual society has its own distinctive functions. The language characteristically used with intimate family and friends, the language generally used with co-workers or
185 neighbors, and the language used with one's bosses or government need not be one and the same. Reading advanced technical or economic material may require literacy in a different language than reading a local gossip column. As long as two or more languages are not rivals for the same societal function, a linguistic division of labor can be both amicable and long-standing. Few English speakers in India, for
190 example, have given up their local mother tongues or their regional languages. Similarly, in Puerto Rico and Mexico, English is typically "a sometime tongue," even among those who have learned it for occupational or educational rewards.

Q There will of course be conflict, not to mention winners and losers. Language conflict occurs when there is competition between two languages for exclusive
195 use in the same power-related function—for example, government or schooling. Most frequently, this friction occurs when one regional or local language seeks to usurp roles traditionally associated with another local tongue. In the Soviet era, Moscow took an aggressive line on local languages, instituting Russian as the sole language of education and government in the Baltics and Central Asia. In the
200 1990s, however, many of these states had slowly deemphasized Russian in schools, government, and even theaters and publishing houses, in favor of their national tongues. Estonia, Latvia, and Lithuania passed the strictest laws, placing education, science, and culture within the exclusive purview of their national languages and (only just recently) leaving ethnic Russian out in the cold.

R Even though local and regional regimes are most likely to use language for political ends, global languages (including English, the language of globalization) can also foster conflict. France's anxiety over the spread of English is well documented. The government in Paris forbids English in advertising and regulates the number of English-language films that may be shown in the country. A cabinet-level official,
210 the minister of culture and communication, is responsible for monitoring the well-being of the national tongue. The Académie Française, France's national arbiter of language and style, approves official neologisms for Anglo-American slang to guard the French language against "corruption." Yet French schools are introducing students to English earlier and earlier.

S Those who speak and master the languages of globalization often suggest that "upstart" local tongues pose a risk to world peace and prosperity. Throughout most of recorded history, strong languages have refused to share power with smaller ones and have accused them of making trouble—disturbing the peace and promoting ethnic violence and separatism. Purging Ireland of Gaelic in the nineteenth century,
220 however, did not convince many Irish of their bonds with England. Those who fear their own powerlessness and the demise of their beloved languages of authenticity have reasons to believe that most of the trouble comes from the opposite end of the language-and-power continuum. Small communities accuse these linguistic Big Brothers of imperialism, linguicide, genocide, and mind control.

T Globalization, regionalization, and localization are all happening concurrently.
They are, however, at different strengths in different parts of the world at any
given time. Each can become enmeshed in social, cultural, economic, and even
political change. English is frequently the language of choice for Tamils in India
who want to communicate with Hindi-speaking northerners. Ironically, for many
230 Tamils—who maintain frosty relations with the central authorities in Delhi—
English seems less like a colonial language than does Hindi. In Indonesia, however,
English may be associated with the military, the denial of civil rights, and the
exploitation of workers, since the United States has long supported Jakarta's
oligarchic regime. Although English is spreading among Indonesia's upper classes,
235 the government stresses the use of Indonesia's official language, Bahasa Indonesia,
in all contact with the general public. Local languages are denied any symbolic
recognition at all. The traditional leadership and the common population in Java,
heirs to a classical literary tradition in Javanese, resent the favoritism shown to
English and Indonesian. Spreading languages often come to be hated because they
240 can disadvantage many as they provide advantages for some.

U English itself is becoming regionalized informally and orally, particularly among
young people, because most speakers today use it as a second or third language.
As students of English are increasingly taught by instructors who have had little
or no contact with native speakers, spoken English acquires strong regional
245 idiosyncrasies. At the same time, however, English is being globalized in the
realms of business, government, entertainment, and education. However, Hindi
and Urdu, Mandarin Chinese, Spanish and vernacular varieties of Arabic can all
expect a boom in these areas in years to come—the result of both a population
explosion in the communities that speak these tongues natively and the
250 inevitable migrations that follow such growth.

V The smallest languages on the world scene will be squeezed between their
immediate regional neighbours on one side and English on the other. Most purely
local languages (those with fewer than a million speakers) will be threatened with
extinction during the next century. As a result, many smaller communities will
255 not only seek to foster their own tongues but also to limit the encroachments of
more powerful surrounding languages. Even in a democratic setting, "ethnolinguistic
democracy" is rarely on the agenda. The US government was designed to protect
the rights of individuals; it is no accident that its founding fathers chose not to
declare an official language. Yet given the vocal opposition to Spanish-language
260 and bilingual education in many quarters of the United States, it seems not
everyone holds the right to choose a language as fundamental.

W What is to become of English? It may well gravitate increasingly towards the
higher social classes, as those of more modest status turn to regional languages
for more modest gains. It might even help the future of English in the long run if
265 its proponents sought less local and regional supremacy and fewer exclusive
functions in the United Nations and in the world at large. A bully is more likely
to be feared than to be popular. Most non-native English speakers may come to

love the language far less in the 21st century than most native English speakers
seem to anticipate. Germans are alarmed that their scientists are publishing
270 overwhelmingly in English. And France remains highly resistant to English in
mass media, diplomacy, and technology. Even as English is widely learned, it
may become even more widely disliked. Resentment of both the predominance of
English and its tendency to spread along class lines could, in the long term,
prove a check against its further globalization.

X There is no reason to assume that English will always be necessary, as it is
today, for technology, higher education, and social mobility, particularly after its
regional rivals experience their own growth spurts. Civilization will not sink into
the sea if and when that happens. The decline of French from its peak of
influence has not irreparably harmed art, music, or diplomacy. The similar
280 decline of German has not harmed the exact sciences. Ancient Greek, Aramaic,
Latin, and Sanskrit—once world languages representing military might,
sophistication, commerce, and spirituality—are mere relics in the modern world.
The might of English will not long outlive the technical, commercial, and
military ascendancy of its Anglo-American power base, particularly if a stronger
285 power arises to challenge it. But just because the use of English around the
world might decline does not mean the values associated today with its spread
must also decline. Ultimately, democracy, international trade, and economic
development can flourish in any tongue.

Y Joshua A. Fishman is Emeritus Distinguished University Research Professor
290 (Social Sciences) at Yeshiva University and visiting professor at Stanford
University (Linguistics and Language Learning and Planning) and New York
University (Educational Psychology).

Source: Fishman, J.A. (1998). The new linguistic order. *Foreign Policy*, *113*, 26–39.